# YOUR EVERYDAY GUIDE TO BEHAVIOURAL FINANCE

# YOUR EVERYDAY GUIDE TO BEHAVIOURAL FINANCE

PRAKASH PRAHARAJ
NIRAKAR PRADHAN

Hay House India
New Delhi • London • Sydney
Carlsbad, California • New York City

**Hay House Publishers (India) Pvt Ltd**
Muskaan Complex, Plot No. 3, B-2, Vasant Kunj, New Delhi – 110070, India

Hay House LLC, P.O. Box 5100, Carlsbad, CA 92018-5100, USA
Hay House UK Ltd, 1st Floor, Crawford Corner, 91-93 Baker Street, London W1U 6QQ, UK
Hay House Australia Publishing Pty Ltd, 18/36 Ralph St., Alexandria NSW 2015, Australia

Email: contact@hayhouse.co.in
Website: www.hayhouse.co.in



First published by Hay House India, 2022
Reprint, 2025
12 11 10 9 8 7 6 5 4 3

ISBN 978-93-91067-66-3 (paperback)
ISBN 978-93-91067-07-6 (ebook)

Printed at Repro India Ltd

FSC www.fsc.org MIX Paper from responsible sources FSC® C047271

Hay House is committed to a sustainable future for our business, our readers and our planet. This book is made from Forest Stewardship Council® certified paper.

The book is dedicated to
our parents, teachers, and clients.

# Contents

# Foreword

One of the bestsellers of 2019, the book *The Man Who Solved the Market: How Jim Simon launched the Quant Revolution* is exclusively devoted to Renaissance Technologies and its founder, Jim Simon. The review on the back-cover of the book carries the message, "No other investor—Warren Buffett, George Soros, or Ray Dalio—can touch the track record of Renaissance Technology founder, Jim Simon. Since 1988, Renaissance Medallion Fund has generated an average annual return of 66% and the firm has recorded trading gains of more than one hundred billion dollars." In June 2020, Financial Times, London, carried the headline in the middle pages, "Top-flight US hedge fund Renaissance shed 20% in a sharp reversal of fortunes."

This reversal was not caused by the inadequacy of the use of technology (Algo, Machine Learning, or Artificial Intelligence), application of various investment theories, or the commitment of team Renaissance or its founder, Jim Simon. It appears to be the result of little less than adequate understanding of the impact of COVID-19 in the likely aggregate behaviour of the investors and intermediaries, monetary and fiscal authorities, managers of businesses, and the society at large on the movement of the capital markets. It is the behaviour of the people that architects trends in capital markets through buy-sell options for the investors and this behaviour is influenced by motivations. The COVID-19 is an unprecedented event in the history of Homo sapiens and thus different sets of persons are reacting differently and in a manner unknown to the history of the capital markets. The warehouse of Renaissance Technologies is probably not able to take any cues from the past learnings because the impact of the COVID-19 is unique and completely unanticipated. Research has revealed that doles remitted by the state to revive consumption is seeping albeit partly into the capital markets and contributing to the quick recovery of the markets after a devastating impact of COVID-19 on the economies across geographies.

Investment management is a science as well as an art. The scientific aspect includes the analysis of the market data—past, present, and propensities applied to various investment theories—to arrive at the options for making investment decisions. The artistic aspect here includes understanding and anticipating the behaviour of all those who influence the market trends following the happening or expectation of dawn of events. It is not only the analysis of past trends but also of expected behaviour in aggregate that leads to future market trends. The application of the art of investment coupled with science leads to better returns. This has given rise to the development of the *Behavioural Theory of Finance*. Capturing the behaviour of individual investors and weaving into investment objectives has given birth to the innovation of Behaviourally Modified Asset Allocation (BMAA). The top-flight investment manager across geographies have been trying to create their own unique fusion of science and art of investment management and securing their place in the top quartile of investment manages by delivering a higher rate of returns consistently.

Investment Management is a serious business. It demands thorough knowledge, deep understanding, continuous evaluation, and total commitment. It also warrants market conduct with agility, alacrity, and action. The profession of investment management has evolved along these lines. Still, even the best amongst the investment managers with a glorious track record like Jim Simon fall sometimes because of inadequate, inaccurate, or inappropriate understanding and action. But that is understood, accepted, and appreciated as the risk of investing and investors are expected to moderate their expectations accordingly. This sentiment is captured in the Vedic philosophy with the phrase—mortals are fallible.

Yet, most individual investors ingrain a fallacious attitude that they know it all and often venture into investing and/or disinvesting directly and also provide clear directions to their investment manager. More often than not, they are gripped by greed or fear and fall prey to hubris and panic in the market. It makes economic sense for individuals to seek support or outsource their investment management to a professional manager. However, it is important for the professional manager entrusted with the responsibilities of being an agent of an investor to understand his principal. The most important aspects to understand are his behaviour, biases, and expectations and then design a BMAA. But the investor can help him understand only if he understands these concepts himself. Thus, the discovery of self—one's own reaction to various events and circumstances—becomes an essential prerequisite for the investor.

## Foreword

The two well-known investment pundits, Mr Prakash Praharaj and Mr Nirakar Pradhan, have learnt the art and science of investment and behavioural finance and used their deep knowledge and understanding as investment managers successfully for decades while working for large well-known financial institutions, and they have come together to document their learnings and experience into a very useful, crisp volume. Currently, they are engaged in designing BMAA for a variety of clients and spreading their learnings as teachers as well. This volume explains in simple terms the theory of behavioural finance and behavioural biases. The book dwells upon all kinds of behavioural biases like availability bias, recency bias, cognitive dissonance bias, endowment bias, self-attribution bias, status quo bias, et al.

The book is a great tool to understand one's own biases and outlines methods to deal with such biases. It shows the path for creating BMAA and suggests methods to deal with them in order to manage and contain risks. The book also facilitates in synchronising the investment portfolio with the life cycle of the investors. The authors use their thesis to create an ideal mix of traditional and behavioural finance when dealing with investments.

I consider this very readable volume worthy of use by the professional investment managers, portfolio advisors, and individual investors.

— Mr G. N. Bajpai
Former Chairman, SEBI
Former Chairman, LIC

# 1

# Introduction

What started as an epidemic in China in late 2019, swiftly morphed into a global pandemic within the next 2-3 months. The virus known as COVID-19 threatened most of the countries by severely impacting global growth in a way never seen in the past. Naturally, the pandemic created volatility in global markets, resulting in a sharp correction in risk assets like equity, commodities, etc. The month of March 2020 saw the Indian equity market losing 23.2 per cent (Nifty 50 index)—the largest monthly decline since October 2008—while midcap stocks fell by 30.3 per cent (Nifty Midcap 100 index).

Economic crises have occurred regularly in the past as we encounter recession almost once in a decade in large developed economies like the USA. Since the economic crisis is reflected in capital markets, volatility is an inevitable factor in equity markets. What is interesting here is to note how investors and markets react to such volatility. As an example, let's have a look at the performance chart of Reliance Industries Limited (RIL), the company enjoying the highest market capitalisation in India.

**RELIANCE INDUSTRIES LTD: STOCK PRICE**
As of 8 June, 2021

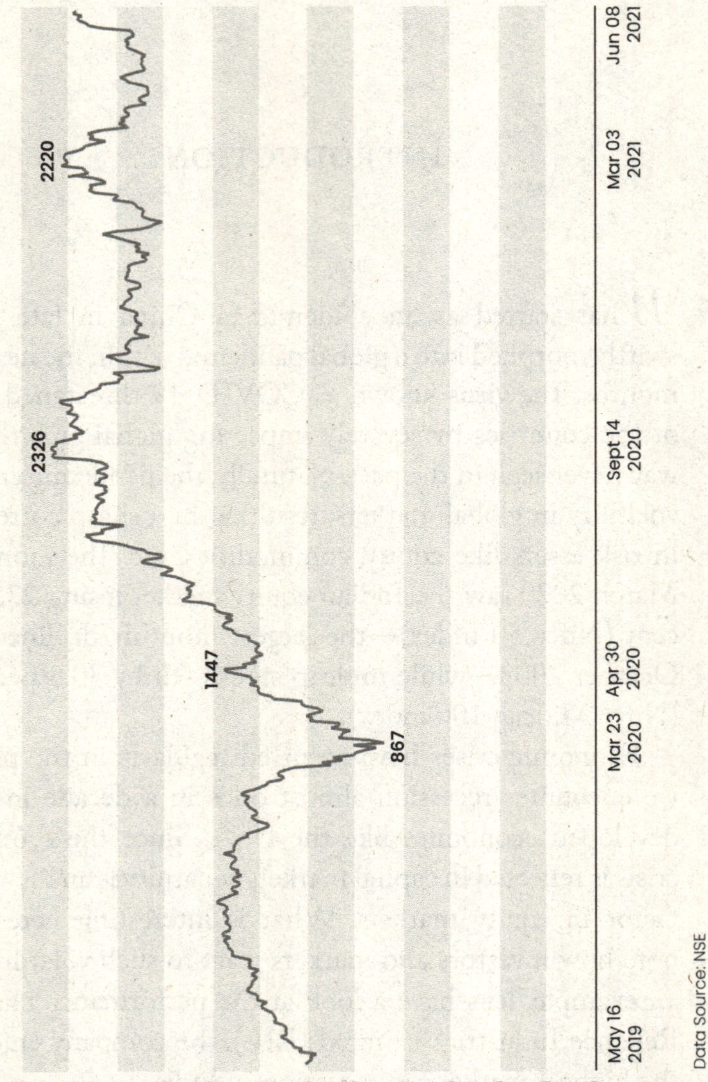

As you would notice from the graph on page 14, during the market crash due to Covid-19, RIL fell by nearly 40% to a 54-week low of INR 867 on March 23, 2020. Many investors sold the shares of RIL in this panic without evaluating the fundamental value of the stock. The investors selling RIL during such a falling market lost about half of their investments. Exactly after a month, i.e., on April 23, 2020, Facebook announced to buy a 9.90% stake in RIL and its stock price went soaring and closed at INR 1,447 on April 30, 2020.

This chronicle of RIL share price that has been demonstrated above is only an example. The point to note here is that investors' behaviour is driven by powerful emotions like fear and greed. More often than not, the investors buy high when everyone else is also buying and they sell at a low level when there is panic in markets. Now let us take a deeper dive to further understand the functioning of markets.

As can be seen from the graph on page 16, crises visit our economies and markets at almost regular intervals. There are a number of studies that indicate that human behaviour to buy high (when everyone else is buying) and selling low (when the market is falling) results in their return from the investments being much lower than the average market return. The distance between what we should do and what we actually do leading to such consistent underperformance in investors' return is aptly called *The Behaviour Gap* by Carl Richards. Behavioural finance, which studies the application of psychology to human decision-making, is currently attracting a lot of attention from market practitioners. It is widely believed that understanding behavioural finance can

**THE 40-YEAR MARKET JOURNEY**

Here are some key milestones that defined the journey of the Sensex over last 40 years

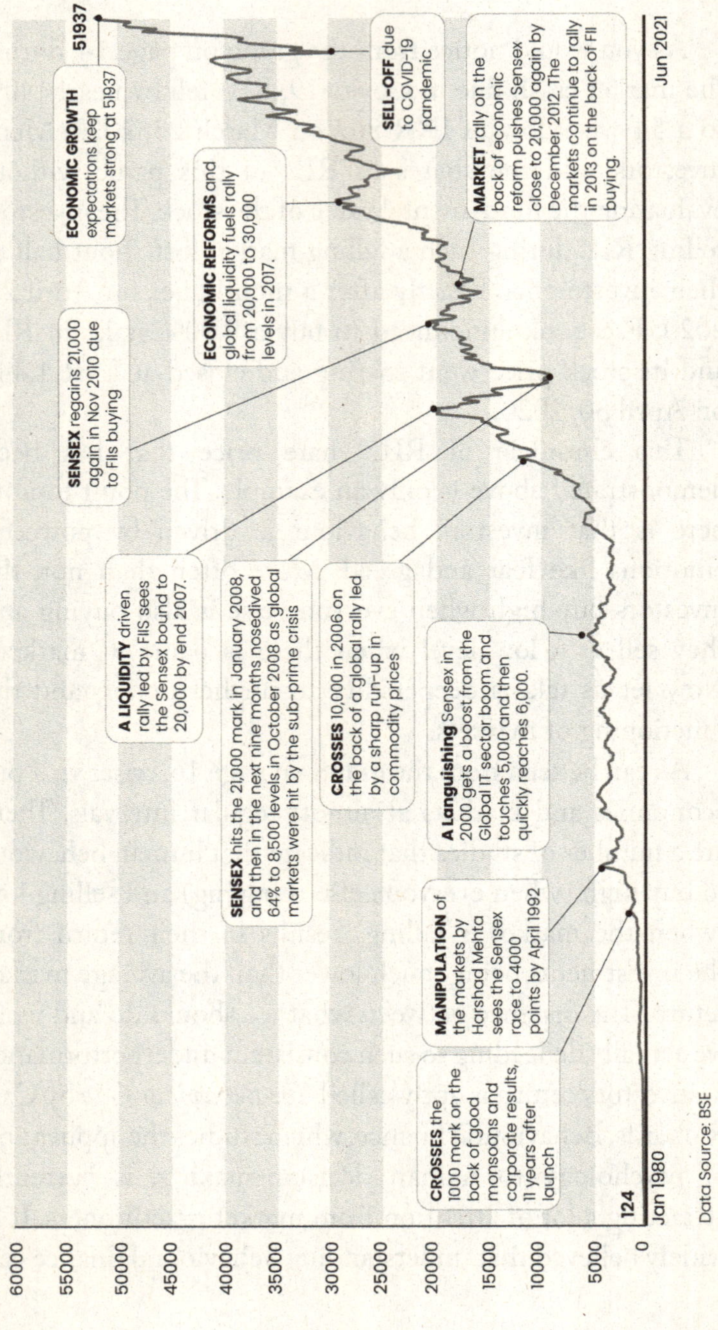

definitely help to avoid emotion-driven decisions that lead to unnecessary losses and thereby enhancing investment successes. For example, a behavioural analysis of RIL in an investor's portfolio could run like the following:

**RIL Stock – Hypothetical Behavioural Analysis**

| Situation | Decision | Behavioural Bias |
|---|---|---|
| In March 2020, COVID-19, creates panic in global markets. | I sold my RIL stock from my portfolio in a falling market. | Loss Aversion. |
| I know RIL is the largest Indian corporate and fundamentally a strong player with robust cash flow and presence in the New Age digital world via Reliance Jio. | I will hold on tc RIL stock. | A prudent investor who manages biases successfully. |
| In April 2020, Facebook announced to buy a 9.90% stake in RIL. This is positive for RIL's business and earnings. RIL stock has risen from a March low of INR 867 to INR 1,400. | I have already lost half of my investments in RIL stock and now the stock has already rallied by by nearly 50% from low. I will avoid buying again. | Regret Aversion. |

## Traditional Versus Behavioural Finance: The Evolving Model

As mentioned before, behavioural finance attempts to understand and explain observed investor and market behaviours. This differs from traditional/standard finance, which is based on the hypotheses about how the investors and markets behave. Traditional finance assumes that people are rational, risk-averse, and well-informed, and that they selfishly act on their own interest (i.e., maximise wealth) without regard to social values. While this framework is appealingly simple, in reality, humans do not act rationally. In fact, humans often act irrationally and in counterproductive, systematic patterns. These deviations from theoretical predictions have paved the way for behavioural finance (BF). It explores how individuals and markets actually behave and focuses on the cognitive and emotional aspects of human behaviour, popularly termed as behavioural biases. It draws on several fields of knowledge, including psychology, sociology, and even biology to investigate the entire gamut of biases. These behavioural biases can broadly be classified into two groups— cognitive and emotional biases.

Cognitive biases or errors stem from basic statistical, information-processing, or memory errors and can be considered as the result of faulty reasoning. On the other hand, emotional biases stem from impulse or intuition and can be considered to result from reasoning influenced by feelings. By understanding such behavioural biases, market practitioners may be able to improve economic outcomes. Once a behavioural bias has been identified, it may be possible to either moderate the bias or adapt to the bias, so that the resulting financial decisions become more acceptable. Thus, an integration of behavioural and traditional finance may lead to superior results.

Behavioural finance influences almost all aspects of the investment process, i.e., investment policy statement, portfolio construction, analyst forecast, client-advisor relationship, decision-making at the committee level, and even market anomalies such as bubbles and crashes. The focus of this book is to place the concepts behind behavioural finance in a simple and intuitive manner for the benefit of a layman. It brings out the dominant biases people face in their daily life; the negative bearings such biases have on investment decision-making, and mitigating strategies to overcome the pitfalls of such biases. Finally, the book ends with real-life case studies which guide the investor on how to construct an optimal portfolio and fulfil long-term financial goals.

## Behaviourally Modified Asset Allocation (BMAA)

BMAA starts with identifying an optimal strategic asset allocation consistent with traditional finance. It then considers the relative wealth of the investor and the nature of the client's biases to adjust that allocation. BMAA considers whether it is better to moderate or adapt to the investor's biases in order to construct a portfolio the investor can stick with. Finally, the amount of deviation from the traditional optimal allocation is determined. This is typically done by setting a range in which the asset class can fluctuate. Thus, BMAA aims at arriving at the best possible practical asset allocation. It integrates both traditional finance (mean-variance optimisation) and behavioural finance (investor's real-life situation) into asset allocation.

**Behavioural Finance: An Indian Perspective**

1. **India's Economy: A promising future**

   Historically, India was the largest economy in the world for most of the two millennia from the 1st until the 19th century (source: Wikipedia). India became one of the poorest countries by the time it became independent from the foreign rule. However, structural economic reforms by successive governments during the last three decades have enhanced India's growth rate.

   Currently, India is the world's fifth-largest economy by nominal GDP and the third largest by purchasing power parity. Since the start of the 21st century, annual average real GDP growth has been 6% to 7%. It took India about 58 years to achieve the first trillion (US$) of GDP growth while the second trillion (US$) was achieved in 7 years and the current GDP of around 2.8 trillion (US$) is expected to double in 6-8 years. Despite the current slowdown, the World Bank has predicted India to be one of the fastest-growing economies ahead.

2. **Indian Capital Market: An engine of wealth creation**

   The gross domestic savings rate of 24.8% during 2001-02 has moved to 30.1% in 2018-19, peaking at 37% in between (Economic Survey, 2020). One-third of India's workers are employed by the services industry, which contributes two-thirds of India's output. The productivity of this segment is made possible by India's shift toward a market economy. With a combined push by both government and private sector, India is undoubtedly one of the world's most vibrant capital markets.

Demat accounts in both NSDL and CSDL put together has crossed the 4 crore mark (NSE). As shown in the graph on page 22, the mutual fund industry's AUM has grown from INR 10.83 trillion as of 31st March 2015 to INR 22.26 trillion as of 31st March 2020, which is more than a two-fold increase in a span of 5 years. India is expected to be the fourth largest private wealth market globally by 2028 (source: www.ibef.org). Falling interest rates on bank deposits, technological transformation facilitating ease of investments, and attractive risk-adjusted returns from the market are driving more and more retail investors to invest in the capital market.

India is evolving to become one of the favoured investment destinations. However, the retail investors in the capital market often lack the knowledge and skills. They suffer from common biases including following the crowd (herd mentality), buying high in a rising market (greed), selling low in a falling market (fear), forecasting the future of the market (anxiety), etc. The rising volatility, the overload of investment tips, and recommendations flowing from television, print, and social media, conferences, investment

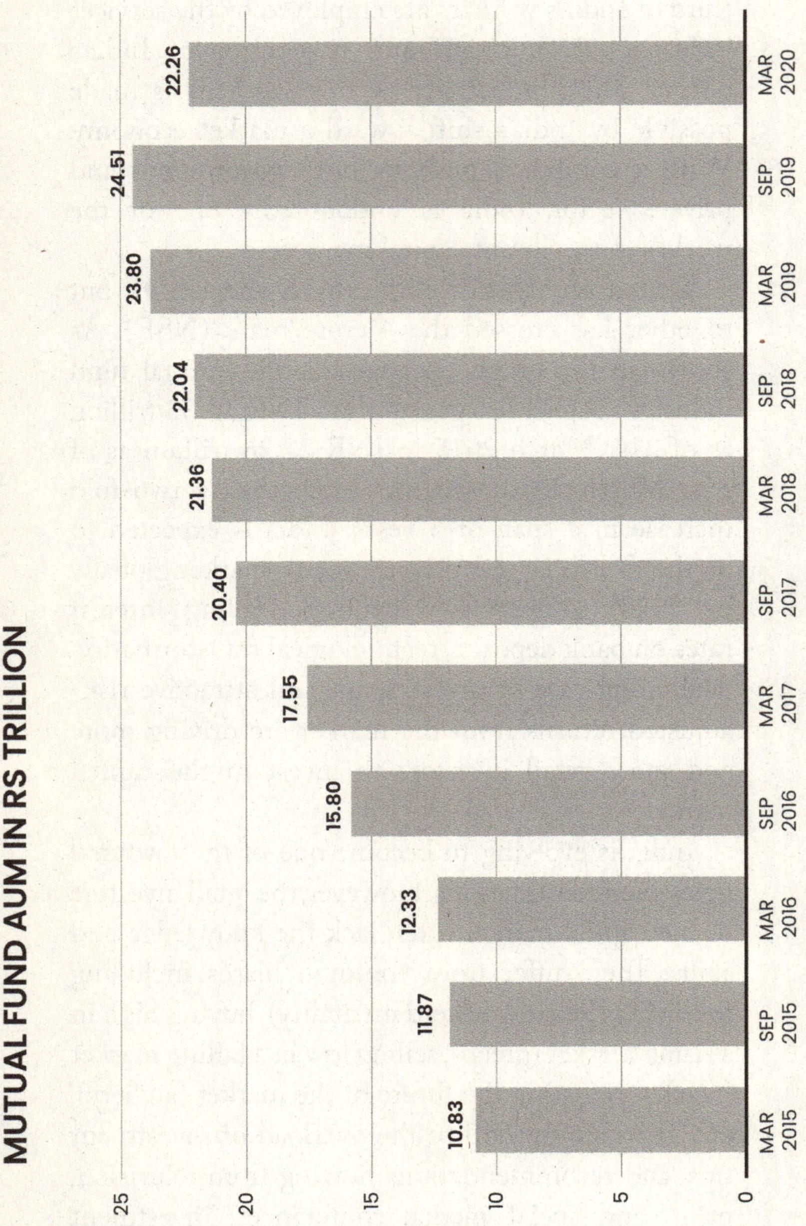


(Data Source: AMFI)

gurus . . . all have added to the confusion. A back-to-basics strategy of drawing up a financial plan, formulating an investment policy/asset allocation, and identifying, assessing, and managing one's own behavioural traits (biases) is the first step on the journey towards investment success.

### 3. Indian Culture: Convergence of spiritual and material wealth

Traditional Indian culture is grounded on ethical and moral values with a focus on generosity, simplicity, and frugality. It seeks to synthesise the material with the spiritual, as aptly illustrated by the concept of four defined goals and four stages of human life. To quote:

धर्मार्थकाममोक्षाख्यं य इच्छेच्छ्रेय आत्मनः ।

Shrimad Bhagwat, Skandha 4, Adhyaya 8, Shloka 41

**Translation:** The four basic pursuits of life, namely *Dharma (righteous conduct)*, *Artha* (wealth accumulation), *Kama (marriage and worldly pleasures)*, and *Moksha* (freedom from all bondages) ensures the well-being of mankind.

The four goals of human life cited above complement the four stages of human life comprising *Brahmacharya* (student), *Grihastha* (householder), *Vanaprastha* (retired), and *Sannyasa* (renunciate). Such clarity in goals at different stages of life emphasises the tenet that each human being can lead a harmonious life balanced by knowledge, health, wealth, happiness, peace, and prosperity without being overwhelmed by the excesses of fear or greed.

**Overcoming Investment Biases**

Looking from an investment perspective, while our knowledge and experiences are about the past, our investment decisions are about the future. Forecasting the future is full of uncertainties and it is decided by a multitude of random variables including economic growth, participants' psyches, governmental/policy measures, global events, weather, demand, supply situations, and so on. While this forecasting is daunting, a balanced approach in the form of strategic asset allocation helps in optimising portfolio performance.

Probably, one of the biggest mistakes an investor can make is ignoring or denying his or her biases. If there are influences that make our decision-making less than objective, then we should learn how to identify and manage these pitfalls and strive to avoid being held captive by them. In the words of Benjamin Graham, one of the brightest investment minds, "In the end, how your investment behaves is much less important than how you behave."

The following chapters provide easy-to-follow guidelines to identify 19 of the major biases as well as manage and control the pitfalls arising from such biases. The key learnings of the book include:

1. Understand human behaviour in investing.
2. Construct a Behaviourally Modified Asset Allocation

(BMAA) and an optimal portfolio addressing individual biases, needs, and preferences while at the same time achieving long-term financial goals.

3. Integrating investment cycle with life-cycle and enjoying the overall journey of life with an integrated perspective of life, values, and investment portfolio regardless of market noises.

## How Will This Book Benefit You?

1. **Investment Advisors:** From a historical perspective, the brokerage or commission-based investing is giving way to a new model where the advisor plays a more crucial role of hand-holding the client and walking through the investment cycle to reach the financial goal. Understanding and applying behavioural finance in the planning, implementation, monitoring, and rebalancing of client portfolios will play a vital role in this process.
2. **Individual Investors:** The book enables individual investors to delve deep into their own behaviours, learn how to modify behaviour and separate their emotions from the decision-making process, create a portfolio, and learn to stick to long-term investment programs to reach long-term financial goals.
3. **Bank Advisors and Portfolio Managers:** Many of the private banks and portfolio managers often add non-traditional asset classes, i.e., venture capital, hedge funds, and other alternative assets to the set of traditional assets like stocks, bonds, and cash.

Including behavioural finance in your repertoire will help the practitioners in adopting a more progressive approach to serving clients.

4. **Consultants:** Consultants to high net-worth individuals, family offices, trusts, or other entities will benefit from this book. Understanding the behavioural tendencies behind clients' investment decisions can positively impact investment choices. And when the investor is happy with the selection of managers from a psychological perspective, it implies that the consultant has done his job well and is likely to keep the client for a longer period.

5. **Students and Researchers:** The behavioural finance sector is receiving considerable attention from the academic world. This introductory book to behavioural finance can be added as a textbook or reference book for students and researchers interested in investments, security analysis, portfolio management, and related areas in business schools and universities.

## 2

# Anchoring and Adjustment Bias

*"Bull markets go to people's head. If you are a duck on a pond, and it is rising due to a downpour, you start going up in the world. But you think it is you, not the pond."*

—Charlie Munger

Anchoring and adjustment is a quite common bias in behavioural finance where the investor estimates a target price or economic value of an object based on the initial information received (anchor or subjective reference point). People often base their decisions on such first source of information they are exposed to (such as stock or real estate) and have difficulty in adjusting their views to new information.

"People make estimates by starting from an initial value that is adjusted to yield the final answer," explained Amos Tversky and Daniel Kahneman in a 1974 paper. "The initial value, or starting point, may be suggested by the formulation of the problem, or it may be the result of a partial computation. In either case, adjustments are typically insufficient. That is, different starting points yield different estimates, which are biased toward the initial values."

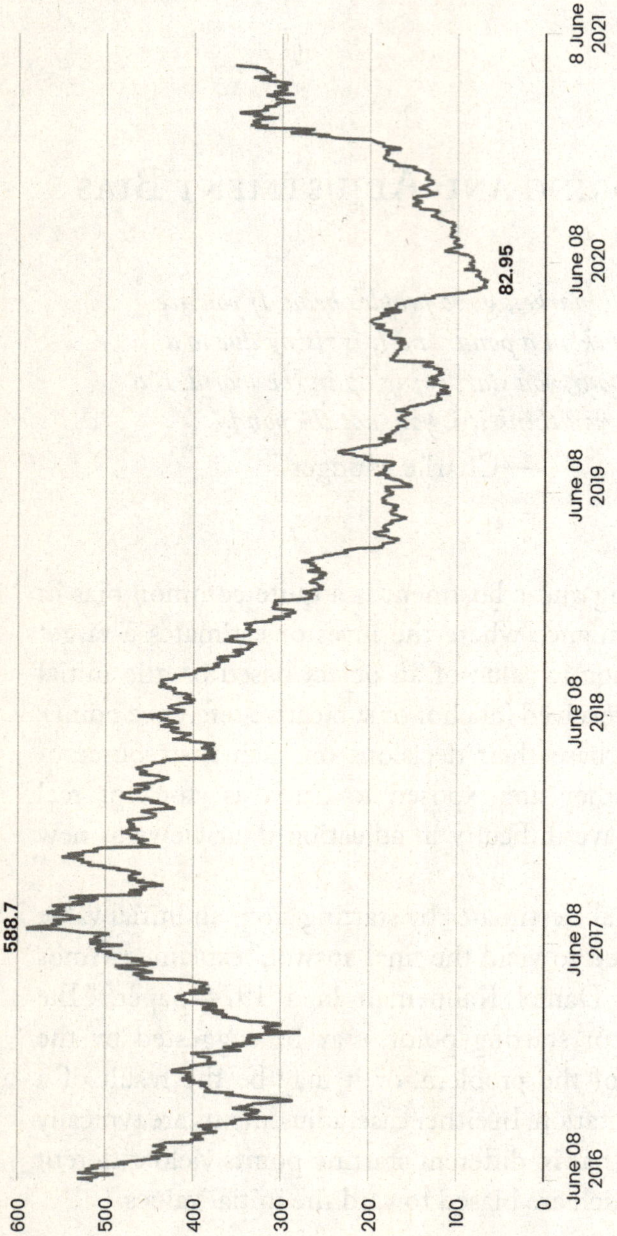


(Data Source: NSE)

Tata Motor Stock Price, 5-Year Chart (As of June 8 2021)

Anchoring and adjustment have been shown to produce erroneous results when the initial anchor deviates from the true value. As an example, let us look at the chart given on page 28.

Suppose you paid INR 308 per share and bought stocks of Tata Motor, way back in 2016. Since then, the stock price went up and nearly doubled to a high of INR 613 in 2017. However, you did not sell the stock but continue to hold. Given the current global economic slowdown, the impact of BREXIT, and ongoing trade tension between the USA and China, the price of the stock has sharply fallen to INR 160 now (see graph on page 28). You know that Tata Motors is the largest Indian commercial automaker and owner of Jaguar Land Rover and thus you are happy to hold the stock in your portfolio. However, the company has posted losses for the last two consecutive quarters. The views from various analysts and media channels are not encouraging. Some analysts have downgraded the stock to 'sell'. Moving forward, the choices before you are as follows:

i. Tata Motor is a big global player. You are confident that the share prices will recover in future towards 600. Hence, you refuse to sell.

ii. The stock is a compelling buy at the current price level of INR 160. There is a huge upside potential as the price may inch up to INR 613. You decide to buy.

iii. Based on sectoral analysis, you observe that the demand for commercial and luxury passenger vehicles from global operations is declining. Both the company's sales and the stock price are falling and exhibiting worsening economic fundamentals. You decide to sell, even though it means a loss of about 50% on your original investment.

iv. You decide to make a more robust top-down fundamental analysis before taking a decision to buy, sell, or hold.

A tendency toward either of the first two responses probably is driven by anchoring and adjustment bias. The stock price has declined about 50% from your purchase price and 74% from the last peak of INR 613. In such scenarios, a rational investor would examine the company's financial situation, make an objective assessment of business fundamentals, and then decide whether to buy, hold, or sell the shares. On the other side, some investors even after going through the loss suffered in the investment and being well aware of worsening fundamentals permit cognitive errors to cloud their judgement and would like to hold on to the stock or make an additional purchase. Decisions not based on fundamentals but driven by past market price in the above case probably reflects anchoring and adjustment bias (anchored to the psychological benchmark of INR 613).

**Impact of Anchoring and Adjustment Bias on Investment**

1. The most notable behaviour witnessed among investors and market players is that they tend to make general market forecasts that are awfully close to the current level. For example, if the NIFTY index is currently at

12,000, then investors are likely to forecast the index in a narrower way than what might be suggested by historical fluctuation. For example, an investor subject to anchoring might forecast the NIFTY to swing between 11,500 to 12,500 at the year-end. (i.e., the corridor ranges between 500 points on either side of the anchor).

2. Investors (and securities analysts) tend to stick too closely to their original estimates when new information is learnt about a company. For example, if an investor determines that next year's earnings estimate is INR 10.00 per share and the company subsequently falters, the investor may not readjust the INR 10.00 figure enough to reflect the change because he or she is 'anchored' to the INR 10.00 figure. This is not limited to downside adjustments; the same phenomenon occurs when companies have upside surprises.

3. Investors tend to make a forecast of the percentage that a particular asset class might rise or fall based on the current level of returns. For example, if the Sensex returned 10 per cent last year, investors will be anchored on this number when making a forecast about next year.

4. Investors can become anchored on the economic states of certain countries or companies. For example. Jet Airways was a bellwether stock for years. Some investors became anchored to the idea that Jet Airways would always be a bellwether. Unfortunately, for some, Jet Airways did not last as a bellwether stock.

## Diagnostic Testing

Ashutosh Gupta, a young finance professional, works for a leading bank in Mumbai. He got married last year and has been living in Navi Mumbai in a rented flat for the last 5 years. After remaining soft for several years, real estate prices have been slowly rising in recent months. Given the lower interest rates for home loans, he is thinking of buying a 2BHK flat. To his enquiry, he receives a call from an agent informing him that a 2BHK flat as per his specifications is available in his neighbourhood. The listed price of the flat is INR 1 crore. Ashutosh is shocked. He knows that barely 3 years ago, the similar flat cost almost half the price, i.e., INR 50 lakhs. Ashutosh tells his agent that he will discuss this with his wife and get back to him shortly. The agent further adds:

1. The demand in the locality has gone up significantly due to the announcement of a new airport proposed to be built in the neighbourhood soon.
2. The demand for real estate property has been going up recently.
3. Ashutosh should decide quickly, as other potential buyers could bid at a higher price.

Knowing these factors, what should Ashutosh do?

1. Offer to bid @ INR 65 lakhs, i.e., 30% increase over INR 50 lakhs (Anchor).
2. Offer to bid @ INR 72.5 lakhs, i.e., 45 % increase over INR 50 lakhs (Anchor).

3. Offer to bid @ INR 80 lakhs, i.e., 60% increase over INR 50 lakhs (Anchor).
4. Offer to bid @ INR 1 crore to be sure to get the deal.

**Test Results Analysis**

The first three responses indicate Ashutosh exhibiting anchoring and adjustment bias. One should remember that the real estate prices have been showing a rising trend. If Ashutosh wants to buy the flat, he should be ready for a higher price. However, a willingness to accept the much higher price level close to INR 1 crore is 100% over anchor price and difficult to accept. Such behaviour can have a significant impact on buying and selling decisions in investment and portfolio management.

**Mitigating Strategies for Anchoring and Adjustment Bias**

The anchoring phenomenon can apply in a multitude of situations. Awareness of one's behavioural tendency of anchoring, considering a range of possible outcomes, expertise, experience, personality, and mood can all modify the effects of anchoring. The following strategies can help to avoid the pitfalls of anchoring and adjustment bias. In fact, the knowledge and awareness of anchoring can also be used for advantage in investment strategies.

1. **Be aware:** Awareness is the best countermeasure to anchoring and adjustment bias. When you are advising clients on the sale or purchase of a security, encourage clients to challenge themselves if the target price or value is anchored to some earlier information.

2. **Research and market forecast:** People often get carried away and estimate the direction of the market or target price for indices/individual securities anchored to the previous year's level. In order to overcome the pitfalls of biased forecasts, one should carry out fundamental research. When it comes to making investment decisions, there are broadly two types of research—macro and micro. Macro research looks mostly at the larger picture of the economy as a whole, i.e., the phase of an economic cycle, interest rates, unemployment, tax rates, government spending, etc. Micro research focuses on specific companies or industries, paying special attention to details like profit margin, debt ratios, stock buybacks, corporate earnings growth, cash flows, price to earnings ratios, etc. Both types of research are required in order to make truly informed decisions while forecasting future market trends and security prices.
3. **Anchoring bias as a tool for negotiation:** The knowledge of anchoring bias can be used to advantage in sales and price negotiations. Many negotiation experts suggest that the participants communicate stiff initial positions (anchor). They believe that an opponent subject to anchoring can be influenced even when the anchor values are extreme. If one party begins a negotiation by offering a given price or condition, then the other party's subsequent counter-offer will likely reflect that anchor. Hence, when negotiating, it is wise to start with an offer much less generous than the figure that reflects your actual position.

4. **Analyst forecasts and market opportunities:** The analysts generally anchor on their initial estimates while issuing upgrades or downgrades. For example, if an analyst is anchored to earnings estimate while earnings are rising, it is likely that the analyst is underestimating the magnitude of the earnings upgrades. Similarly, if an analyst is anchored to earnings estimate while earnings are falling, it is likely that the analyst is underestimating the magnitude of the earnings downgrades. A sophisticated investor with knowledge of anchoring and adjustment bias could benefit by taking advantage of the gap between the analyst forecasts and actual market price movements

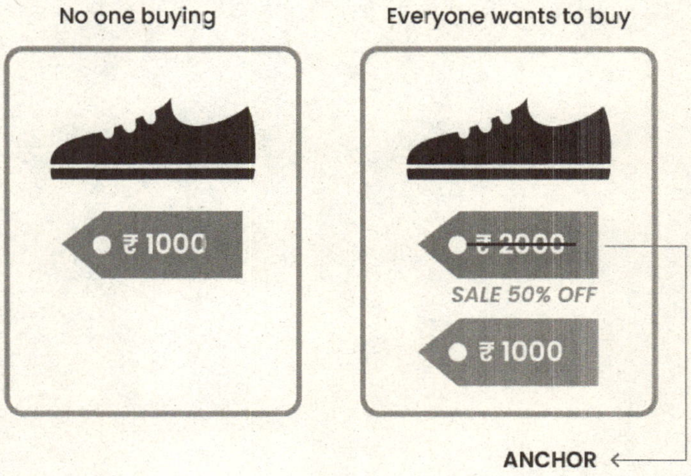


A pair of shoes priced at INR 2,000/- with a discount of 50% will have more buyers than a pair quoted at INR 1,000/- without any discount. The anchor set at INR 2,000 influences the decision.

# 3

# Availability Bias

*"Never ask the barber if you need a haircut."*
—Warren Buffet

There is an old saying, 'All that glitters is not gold' which implies that not everything that looks precious or true turns out to be so. This concept can be applied to availability bias. People having availability bias normally adopt a heuristic (sometimes called a rule of thumb or a mental shortcut) approach to decision-making. Here, the decisions are made based on readily available information that is more recent and memorable. Easily recalled outcomes are often perceived as being more likely to come to fruition than those that are harder to recall or understand. Looking beyond what is readily available requires some amount of effort which people tend to avoid. Let us take a closer look to understand this better.

During the period 2003-07, Indian markets witnessed a bull run buoyed by several favourable factors like easy liquidity, cheap credit, low-interest rates, excessive leverage, and healthy foreign portfolio inflows. There was considerable exuberance created by market intermediaries, especially by the steadily expanding mutual funds and insurance industry. A large number of first-time retail investors entered into Indian stock market during the last leg of the bull run (2007-08). Unfortunately, the Indian stock market crashed in 2008-09, in line with global markets during this period popularly known as global financial crisis (GFC). Events like the collapse of Lehman Brothers created fear and panic in Indian markets. A large number of those first-time investors lost confidence in the market and sold their stocks in a falling market and, thereby lost more than half of their wealth. However, the investors who kept faith in the market (not moved by bias) and continued their investments were not only able to save their investments but also gained as markets recovered in about a year's time.

The Indian insurance industry was opened up to the private sector in 2001. For the next 10 years, i.e., during the period 2001-2010, a hybrid product called ULIP (Unit Linked Insurance Policy) that combines insurance and investment witnessed significant interest from the investors. The investments, both equity and debt are market linked. Investors got heavily influenced by a wave of high-pitched advertisements and bought ULIPs without proper due diligence and later on, suffered heavy losses. Here below are a few examples:

**Example 1:** Unit Linked Insurance Policy (ULIP) is similar to bank Fixed Deposit (FD).

**What they say:** ULIPs work like a bank FD and since it comes with insurance cover, they are better than an FD. When pitching the ULIP, the illustration benefit is prepared at a yield of 4 and 8 per cent, which is comparable to what the investor earns on FDs. However, this works in the ULIP's favour since the returns from FDs are subject to tax incidence whereas ULIPs are tax free, which means the post-tax return from bank FDs is lower than ULIPs.

**What it really means:** In ULIPs, a part of the premium is allocated towards cost of life cover and the rest is assigned to a common pool of money called fund, which invests in equity, debt, or a combination of both. The returns on the investment depend upon the performance of the underlying fund. In the example above, ULIPs (debt funds) are being compared with bank FD.

A fixed deposit is the preferred saving option for many Indians as it provides high safety, a relatively shorter time horizon, and guaranteed rate of return with capital preservation. ULIPs, on the other hand, are subject to lock in period of 5 years and includes cost of life cover. Besides, the return from ULIPs is market linked and there is no assured return as in case of bank FD. Thus, bank FD differs significantly from ULIPs in terms of liquidity, costs of insurance, risk, and return.

**Example 2:** ULIP is a 5-year tax-saving product.

**What they say:** "You have to invest for only five years"—this is a common sales pitch used to attract potential buyers who are merely looking to save tax and lock in funds for a short duration.

**What it really means:** ULIPs have a lock-in period of five years, but it doesn't mean one has to exit after that tenure. As costs are front-loaded in ULIPs and the majority of the charges are levied in the initial five years, exiting after the lock-in may not be financially efficient. ULIPs are meant to be long-term investments and exit after 5-year works to the investor's disadvantage.

**Example 3:** Double your money from ULIPs.

**What they say:** Invest in ULIP and get your money doubled in five years.

**What it means:** Such a common sales pitch is popular especially in times when the stock market is at a high. Past returns of ULIPs (equity fund) are shown to prospective buyers to lure them in. One may choose to invest in equity, debt, or both in a ULIP. The returns will depend on the underlying performance of each asset class (equity or bonds) of the fund option. There is no guarantee that the fund will generate a specific return or provide an assured amount. The fund value on maturity will be a function of the number of units held and the NAV of the fund option as of that date. If the market rises, so will the fund value and vice versa.

So, a deeper analysis reveals:

1. ULIP is fundamentally different from bank fixed deposits.
2. ULIP is not merely a 5-year tax-saving product and essentially requires commitment for a longer time horizon.
3. ULIP is not a suitable product for a person looking purely for investment. In such a case, one should probably opt for a mutual fund rather than ULIP.

## Impact of Availability Bias on Investments

People inadvertently overestimate the importance of readily available information. They assume that readily available thoughts and ideas examined in the light of impressions drawn from past experience represent unbiased indicators of statistical probabilities. Each variation of availability bias has unique implications in personal finance, both for advisors and clients. This includes:

1. **Readily available information driving investment decisions:** Investors choose investments based on readily available information. Their decisions get easily influenced by high-impact advertisements or suggestions received from advisors, friends, etc. They follow the rules of thumb or other shortcuts. They are not inclined to engage in serious research or due diligence to validate if the investment selected indeed fits into their financial plan. Such behaviour often leads to suboptimal investments. For example, an investor might be investing in low-performing but heavily advertising mutual fund, while ignoring high-performing mutual fund with low or no advertisements.
2. **Geographical boundaries to the investment universe:** Investors choose investments based on self-made categorical lists available in their memory. In their minds, other categories will not be easily recalled and, thus, will be ignored. For example, Indian investors may readily categorise India as the best investment destination and readily invest in

Indian markets. However, they may ignore many attractive investment opportunities available abroad because investment in those countries doesn't get recalled naturally in their memory.

3. **Psychological boundaries to the investment universe:** Investors are normally inclined to choose investments that fit into their limited experiences. They would be ready for investment in the industry they are familiar with, the region they live in, or the community they normally interact with. For example, investors who work in the banking and finance sector may irrationally believe that banking and finance stocks are the most profitable investments, while at the same time ignore similar or much better investment opportunities available in other sectors.

4. **Portfolios tuned to personal preferences:** Investors choose investments that match their personality traits or preferences. They usually ignore potentially good investments because they can't naturally relate to the characteristics of those investments. For example, many Indians are thrifty by nature. They invest their savings in bank deposits. The real returns from bank deposits are suboptimal when looking from a long-term perspective. However, considering the comfort of safety, Indian investors prefer to place their money in low-return bank deposits. They may not be inclined to even look at inexpensive value stocks with much higher return potential when compared to traditional bank deposits.

**Diagnostic Testing**

The following questions are designed to detect cognitive errors stemming from availability bias. To complete the test, select the option that best characterises your response to each item.

**Question 1:** Suppose you have some money to invest and you hear about an IPO (Initial Public Offer) in the telecom sector being launched. Your neighbour who is known to have a good stock market sense recommends you invest in IPO shares. What is your response to this situation?

a) I will likely buy some shares because my neighbour is usually right about these things.

b) I will likely talk to other analysts and do further research before deciding.

**Question 2:** Suppose that you are planning to buy banking stock. Your friend has sent you a report on bank X and you like the story. While you are going to purchase 100 shares of bank X, you hear about a popular financial news showing that another bank (bank Y) has just released very good quarterly results. In such a case, how would you respond?

a) I will likely take this information as confirmation that the banking sector is favourably placed and I will go ahead with the purchase of bank X.

b) I will pause before buying any share and request for a research report on both the banks to do a fundamental analysis before buying the stock.

c) I will purchase bank Y rather than wait as bank Y appears to be hot stock and I don't like to miss the opportunity.

**Test Results Analysis**

Question 1: Respondents choosing option 'a' are likely to be susceptible to availability bias.

Question 2: Respondents choosing option 'c' are likely to be susceptible to availability bias.

**Mitigating Strategies for Availability Bias**

The following strategies can help investors to mitigate the pitfalls of availability bias:

1. The important step is to be aware of pitfalls of availability bias by adopting an attitude of continuous learning, research, and homework.
2. The investors should not blindly go with the popular advertisements and advices from friends and family members and succumb to 'flavour of the season'.
3. The investor should take investment decisions from a medium- to long- term perspective rather than chasing short-term trends.
4. The investor should be open to broader inputs, differing views, and contrarian perspectives before taking a call on investments. A geographical, industrial, and sectoral diversification will make the portfolio move away from the suboptimal performance arising out of availability bias.

# 4

# Representativeness Bias

*"The question is not what you look at but what you see."*
—Henry Thoreau

The representativeness heuristic was first described by psychologists Amos Tversky and Daniel Kahneman during the 1970s. Like other heuristics, making judgements based on representativeness is intended to work as a type of mental shortcut, allowing us to make decisions quickly. Representativeness bias occurs when the similarity in objects or events confuses people's thinking regarding the probability of an outcome. People frequently make the mistake of believing that two similar things or events are more closely correlated than they actually are.

Making decisions based on representativeness involves comparing an object or situation to the schemas or mental prototypes that people already have in mind. Such schemas are based on past learning, but can also change as a result of new learning. If an existing schema doesn't adequately account for the resulting situation, it can lead to poor judgements. Let's see some real-life examples of representativeness bias:

- **Jurors and criminal justice:** Jurors can be inundated with vast amounts of information. Sometimes, faced with the complex and ambiguous nature of many judgements as well as the pressure of time, legal decision-makers may make judgements about guilt based on how closely a defendant matches their prototype of a 'guilty suspect' or how well the crime represents a certain crime category.
- **Doctors and healthcare:** Doctors and healthcare professionals may make diagnostic and treatment decisions based on how well a patient and their symptoms match an existing prototype. Unfortunately, this can lead professionals to overestimate similarity and ignore other relevant information.
- **Election and political choices:** Representativeness can play a role in how people vote and the candidates they support. For example, a person might support a political candidate because they fit the mental image of someone they think is a great leader without really learning about that person's platform.
- **Work and social relationships:** Representativeness can affect the judgements we make in the workplace or when meeting new people. It may lead us to form inaccurate impressions of others. For example, in one study, researchers found that managers made biased decisions more than 50% of the time, many of which were based on representativeness.

In the context of financial investments, there are two primary interpretations of representativeness bias applicable to individual investors.

1. **Base-Rate Neglect:** In base-rate neglect, some investors tend to rely on stereotypes when making investment decisions. For example, investors attempt to determine the potential success of, say, an investment in company X by contextualising the venture in a familiar, easy-to-understand classification scheme. Such an investor might categorise company X as a 'value stock' and draw conclusions about the risks and rewards that follow from that categorisation. This reasoning, however, ignores other unrelated variables that could substantially impact the success of the investment. Investors often embark on this erroneous path because it looks like an alternative to the diligent research required when evaluating an investment.

   **Example:** Sunita, an investor, hears through a friend about a forthcoming IPO being issued by ABC, a pharmaceutical company. There is a lot of hype in the market about this IPO. A few brokers have issued a 'buy' rating on the stock. Sunita is quite excited and she places an order for 500 shares through her broker.

   **Analysis:** Several studies have shown that a very low percentage of IPOs turn out to be good long-term investments. The common investor preference for IPOs is likely since investors in hot IPOs usually make money in the first few days after the offering. Over time, however, these stocks tend to trail their IPO prices, often never returning to their original levels. By ignoring relevant statistics and probabilities and not doing in-depth research and analysis, one might fall prey to base-rate neglect.

**Advice for Base-Rate Neglect**

Referring to the earlier example of Sunita investing in a hot IPO, she should stop and ask herself, "What is the probability that stock ABC will fail?" To make a sound decision regarding her investment, it is vital for Sunita to go back and do some more research to determine if the above IPO merits investment based on both top-down/bottom-up fundamental analysis.

2. **Sample-Size Neglect:** In sample-size neglect, investors, when judging the likelihood of a particular investment outcome, often fail to accurately consider the sample size of the data on which they base their judgements. They incorrectly assume that small sample sizes are representative of populations. Some researchers call this phenomenon *the law of small numbers*. The small sample that the individual has examined may not be representative of the data at large.

**Example:** Geeta, an investor, talks to a stockbroker whose firm employs an analyst who appears to have made many recent successful stock picks. From the discussion, she learns that all the three stocks recommended by the analyst have appreciated about 15% during the last six months. Sunita decides to buy all three stocks for her portfolio.

**Analysis**: Geeta can make significant financial errors if she takes investment decisions based solely on a limited data sample, i.e., decision based on only a few recommendations. She should ask for more data for consideration in order to avoid missing out on any important piece of information that could impact her investments. For example, the same broker/analyst team might have made several losing recommendations during the previous year.

### Advice for Sample-Size Neglect

Similarly, in the earlier example of Geeta, she might conclude that the analyst possesses remarkable skill based on the performance recommendation over the past six months. Viewed in the context of the thousands of analysts, an important question that Geeta should consider is: "Is the six-month track record of an analyst a sheer luck or an indication of skill?"

## Mitigating Strategies for Representative Bias

1. The investor should maintain records of all investment decisions supported by reasoning behind such decisions. There should be periodically matching of the investment rationale with the actual outcomes for learning and future guidance.
2. The investor should implement long-term asset allocation strategy and create a diversified portfolio.

One should avoid chasing short-term performance and excessive trading.

3. One should ask questions like the following before making investment in funds:

    - How does the proposed investment compare to the funds of similar size and style?
    - Have there been changes in the managers of the portfolios?
    - What is the general reputation of the manager?
    - Has the portfolio manager changed their style or investment approach due to the changing conditions?

# 5

# Framing Bias

*"The mind is its own place and in itself, can make a heaven of hell, a hell of heaven."*

—John Milton

The above eloquent and insightful lines from John Milton exposes the frailties of the human mind. It reflects how framing affects what we notice, how we weigh our choices, how we deliberate, and ultimately, how we decide and behave.

Framing bias occurs when one's decision is based on the way the information is presented (example, framed through wordings, settings, or situations) as opposed to just on the facts themselves. The same facts presented in two different ways can lead to people making different judgements or decisions. In behavioural finance, people have the tendency of deciding on options based on whether the options are presented with a positive or negative connotation, i.e., as a gain or as a loss. Research in behavioural finance shows financial decisions can be wildly influenced by framing.

## Examples of Framing Bias

1. Here is a classic example of visual framing. Which of the following horizontal lines is the longest?

(Source: Wikipedia.org)

If your eyes lead you to believe that the middle line is the longest, you have been deceived. In fact, all the lines are of the same length.

2. Let us take a look at the following earnings reporting:

   - **Option 1:** "In Q2, Earnings per Share (EPS) of XYZ was INR 12.50 compared to expectations of INR 13.00."
   - **Option 2:** "In Q2, Earnings per Share (EPS) of XYZ improved to INR 12.50 compared to INR 12.00 in Q1."

   Clearly, option 2 highlighting the improvement of earnings over the previous quarter brings a positive impetus in reporting and does a better job of framing.

3. Twice as many people will opt for surgery where the proposition states "There is a chance that 90 per cent of patients will be saved" versus "There is a chance that 10 per cent of patients will die".

## Impact of Framing Bias on Investments

1. The investors could be frame-dependent due to their restricted ability to absorb the excess information in complex learning environments. Often, the irrational approach of the individuals could lead them to exercise negative investment behaviours. Depending on the way questions are set up, they may respond either conservatively or aggressively. Optimistically worded questions are more likely to garner positive responses. Similarly, optimistically worded answer choices are more likely to be selected than the pessimistically phrased alternatives.
2. Narrow framing, a subset of framing bias, refers to a tendency to see specific investments in isolation without considering the context of the overall portfolio. It can cause even long-term investors to obsess over short-term market fluctuations in a single industry or stock. Focusing only on short-term market fluctuations may lead to excessive trading and thus may contribute to below optimal portfolio performance.
3. Sometimes, framing and loss aversion can work together to explain aggressive behaviour from the investor. For example, an investor who has incurred a net loss could very likely select a riskier investment, whereas a net gainer feels predisposed toward less risky alternatives.

### Diagnostic Testing

The wording or language used has the potential to make a difference to the investor's decision-making. Here below are two diagnostic questions.

**Question 1:** Suppose that you are evaluating two funds ABC and XYZ for investment. Over the past ten years, ABC has had an average annual return of 8 per cent, with a standard deviation of 12 per cent. You can expect two-thirds of all returns to fall between -4 per cent and 20 per cent. On the other hand, during the same investment horizon, one can expect 95 per cent of returns from XYZ to fall between -16 per cent and 32 per cent. Which fund is better?

a) Fund ABC because the expected downside is only 4% compared to the expected loss of 16% from XYZ.
b) Fund XYZ because the expected upside is 32%, much higher than 20% from ABC.

**Question 2:** Suppose you are preparing for retirement. You need INR 500,000 annually to live comfortably, but you could take care of basic needs for about INR 400,000 and could even survive on a minimum of INR 300,000 if necessary. Now, imagine that you are choosing between two hypothetical investment options. Option 1 guarantees you an income of INR 400,000 per year—offering you a chance at leading a risk-free lifestyle. On the other hand, Option 2 offers you a 50 per cent chance of earning INR 500,000 and a 50 per cent chance of receiving INR 300,000 each year. Which option would you choose—option 1 or option 2?

**Test Results Analysis**

Question 1: People who respond to invest either in ABC or XYZ, considering the differing risk and returns parameters between the two funds, are likely to be subject to framing bias. In fact, both the options assume the same average annual return and standard deviation.

Question 2: Investors subjected to framing bias will probably prefer an assured income in option 1 in comparison to the riskier option 2. This is because option 1 is framed in a relatively positive fashion, focusing on the guaranteed (safe) return. The framing in Question 2, however, is less upbeat but also provides a similar return of INR 400,000 (mean return). As both the investment options offer the same risk-adjusted return, the investor preferring either option over the other is likely to be suffering from framing bias.

**Mitigating Strategies for Framing Bias**

Human behaviour is frame-dependent. Frame dependence stems from a mix of cognitive and emotional factors. The emotional aspects pertain to how people feel as they register information. On the other hand, the cognitive aspects relate to how people organise information mentally. Here below are a few suggested strategies to overcome framing bias.

1. **Portfolio perspective:** The first and most important strategy in mitigating the pitfalls of framing bias is to have a portfolio perspective. In this context, the strategic asset allocation designed to satisfy

investor's long-term objectives and constraints assumes crucial importance. Any investment decision being contemplated should conform to the guidelines of strategic asset allocation prescribed in IPS (Investment Policy Statement).

2. **Avoid short-term trading:** Investors engaging in narrow framing may become preoccupied with short-term market movements in a particular stock or industry. They may favour certain asset classes while remaining oblivious to others. Several studies point to the fact that such term trading involves significant cost and contributes to long-term portfolio underperformance. One should focus on overall wealth accumulation and long-term financial goals through strategic asset allocation irrespective of market volatilities.

3. **Loss aversion:** Under normal circumstances, investors avoid losses and prefer gains. However, under specific situations when investors feel that they have been faring poorly, they will seek out risks to compensate for the losses incurred. This is where the role of advisors plays a crucial role. The advisor needs to carefully advise the client on how to address investment decisions objectively with a portfolio perspective.

4. **Research reports:** Analysts' research reports often come with a lot of opinion and bias included in the research. There will always be the point where the data can be made to look positive or negative. It is the investors who have to ask themselves how

reasonable their comparison is and how biased their decision will be based on the presented data. The key is to remove any editorial/judgemental comments and look at only the key numbers and underlying assumptions driving the valuation. One should carefully analyse such information to arrive at own conclusions, rather than being swayed by how the information is presented.

5. **Framed questions:** Risk tolerance questionnaires are administered for ascertaining client goals and selecting appropriate investments. Advisors and practitioners need to ensure that the questions are based on facts. The answers and choices in the questionnaire need to be as objective as possible, keeping in view the client's long-term goals and strategic asset allocation.

# 6

# Conservatism Bias

*"Don't be afraid of change. You may lose something good, but you may gain something better."*

—The Buddha

Conservatism bias is a mental process in which people emphasise the pre-existing information, views, or forecasts over the new data. This can make investors and analysts slow to react to new critical information and place too much weight on the original set of information. According to various research reports, people tend to cling to a view or forecast. Once a position has been stated, most analysts and investors find it hard to move away from that view, and when the movement does occur, it happens very slowly.

## Examples of Conservatism Bias

Suppose that an investor has consistently invested in the stocks of a reputed Fortune 500 company posting excellent annual profits in excess of 10 per cent. Subsequently, the investor receives negative news regarding the company's earnings being significantly impacted due to trade related conflict between economic superpowers. This news contradicts another positive earnings estimate received the previous month. Conservatism bias may cause the investor to *underreact* to the new information, maintaining impressions derived from the previous estimate rather than acting on the updated information.

It may be mentioned that the conservatism bias may appear to conflict with representativeness bias. In representativeness, people overreact to new information whereas in conservatism, people underreact to the new information. In fact, people can exhibit both biases as well.

**Research Review**

In the field of behavioural finance, researchers seek to understand how human behaviour and psychology influences the way prices are set in financial markets. It is widely observed that investors normally overreact or underreact to news, thereby leading to market anomalies.

i. **Investor Overreaction**

   Suppose that a company announces positive news that their earnings reports have been consistently above expectations over the period of three to five years. It is highly possible that the investors might overreact to such news and become excessively optimistic about the company's prospects, pushing its stock price to unnaturally high levels. In the subsequent years, however, this trend might not persist, making investors realise that they were unduly optimistic about the business and the stock price may correct subsequently.

ii. **Investor Underreaction**

Several research studies point to the fact that investors sometimes make the mistake of underreacting to certain types of financial news. For example, suppose a company announces quarterly earnings that are substantially higher than expected. The evidence suggests that investors see this as good news and send the stock price higher but, for some reason, not high enough. Over the next six months, this mistake is gradually corrected as the stock price slowly moves upward towards the level it should have attained at the time of the announcement. Investors who buy the stock immediately after the announcement will benefit from this upward drift and enjoy higher returns.

The same underreaction principle applies to bad news. If bad news, like a company cutting its dividend, is announced, then the stock price will fall. However, it might not fall enough at the time of the announcement and instead, continues to drift downward for several months. In both cases, when investors are faced with either good or bad announcements, they initially underreact to this news and only gradually incorporate its full import into the stock price.

## Impact of Conservatism Bias on Investments

1. **Sticking to original view:** Conservatism bias can cause investors to stick to original forecast and under-weigh emerging new information. For example, assume an investor purchases a security based on the knowledge that the company is going

to benefit from a proposed merger. Subsequently, the merger fails to fructify. The investor may still cling to the initial, optimistic report and may fail to act on the updated negative announcement.

2. **Underreaction:** The conservatism-biased investors underreact to new information. For example, the investor may not quickly respond to the corporate announcements that have a significant impact on the company stock, such as earnings, dividend, stock splits, etc. If the announcement has a negative impact on the stock, the bias may cause investor not to take a timely decision and lose money as the stock price falls.
3. **Inaction in the face of complex situations:** Sometimes, companies resort to many policy changes (for example, change of accounting relating to depreciation), resulting in significant changes to business and income. Rather than understanding and assessing the impact of such changes on the company's performance, the investor suffering from conservatism bias may continue the prior positive view about the company.

## Diagnostic Testing

The following questions can help to detect elements of conservatism bias. To complete the test, select the option that best characterises your response to each item.

**Question 1:** Suppose, you have invested in the stocks of a leading Indian pharma company having significant exports to the USA. You hear the news that the US FDA (Food and Drug Administration) has commenced inspection of the company's manufacturing units. Such inspections require significant attention, time, and resources and often impact overall sales and earnings. What is your natural reaction to this information?

a) I tend to ignore such information because I have already made the investment. I have determined that the company will be able to come out successful eventually.
b) I will re-evaluate my reasons for buying the stock, but I will probably stick with it because I usually stick with my original ideas.
c) I will re-evaluate my reasoning for buying the stock and will decide, based on an objective consideration of all the facts, whether or not to exit the investment.

**Question 2:** You own a particular stock. Then comes news with potentially negative implications for the price of a stock. How quickly do you react to such information?

a) I usually wait for the market to communicate the significance of the information and then I decide what to do.
b) Sometimes, I wait for the market to communicate the significance of the information, but other times, I respond without delay.
c) I always respond without any delay.

**Test Result Analysis**

People choosing option 'a' or 'b' to any of the above questions indicates susceptibility to conservatism bias.

**Mitigating Strategies for Conservatism Bias**

1. **Awareness is the key:** Conservatism is a cognitive (information processing) bias. Advice and continuing education can often correct or reduce the adverse impact of such bias. Specifically, investors must first avoid clinging to any kind of forecasts or predictions. They must also make sure to react decisively to any kind of new information.
2. **Review new information:** Once the new information is received, the investor should ask questions like: 'How does this impact the original forecast?' and 'Does this have a negative impact on my investment?' It is important to understand that hanging on to a view can become detrimental, simply because 'your view' might lead to a negative outcome and cause much grief.
3. **Prepare a checklist for investment decision:** Another suggested strategy to overcome the bias is to prepare a checklist containing say the top five relevant factors that you believe should drive your decision to invest or not to invest. For example, the checklist for investing in equities could cover questions on the price-to-earnings ratio (P/E), price-to-book value (P/BV), price-to-cash flow ratio, current ratio, debt-to-equity ratio, gross profit margin, net profit margin, etc. Such a structured

approach would help in keeping emotions separate from the investment decision-making process.

4. **Professional advice:** Investors should seek professional advice when trying to interpret any information that they have difficulty in understanding.

# 7

# Confirmation Bias

*"I don't always know what I'm talking about,
but I know I'm right."*

—Muhammad Ali

In the world of investing, confirmation bias leads investors to seek out information that supports their original idea rather than to look for information that contradicts it. As a result, this bias can often lead to flawed decisions because one-way information can distort investors' reference points, leaving them with an incomplete picture of the situation.

Confirmation bias can be thought of as a form of selection bias where decision-makers observe, overvalue, or actively seek out information that confirms their claims, while simultaneously ignore or devalue evidence that might discount their claims.

**Examples of Confirmation Bias**

1. An investor hears a rumour that a company is on the verge of declaring bankruptcy. Based on this information, the investor considers selling the stock. When they go online to read the latest news about the company, they read only the stories that confirm the likely bankruptcy scenario and miss a story

about a new product the company has just launched that is expected to perform well and increase sales. Instead of holding the stock, the investor sells it at a substantial loss just before it turns around and climbs to an all-time high.

2. A teacher believes that the girl students are doing better in academics nowadays. He quotes the percentage of girls scoring more than 90% in CBSE 12th exam for this. Another teacher who believes boys are doing better will quote the percentage of boys getting selected in the main IIT examination to prove his belief that boys are better in academics.

3. Let us consider the debate over gun control. Suppose Mr X is in support of gun control. He seeks out news stories and opinion pieces that reaffirm the need for limitations on gun ownership. When he hears stories about shootings in the media, he interprets them in a way that supports his existing beliefs. On the other hand, Mr Y is opposed to gun control. He seeks out news sources that are aligned with his position. And when he comes across news stories about shootings, he interprets them in a way that supports his current point of view. So even though both Mr X and Mr Y read the same story, their bias tends to shape the way they perceive the details in a way that confirms their respective beliefs.

**Impact of Confirmation Bias on Investments**

A few investment mistakes arising from confirmation bias are listed below:

1. A person with confirmation bias only seeks out information that confirms their pre-existing beliefs about an investment that they have made and avoids information that may contradict their beliefs. This behaviour can cause investors to make poor decisions, both in terms of long-term investments and short-term trading bets.
2. Confirmation bias can cause employees to over concentrate in a company's stock and ignore basic principles of portfolio diversification. IBM and other examples demonstrate that intraoffice buzz about company's prospects lead to indiscriminate reliance by employees on the company's stock. The fact remains that employees believe the companies they are working will do well.
3. Confirmation bias can cause investors to hold on to under-diversified portfolios. Over many years, some investors accumulate a large position in identified preferred stock. Such a concentration results in a lopsided portfolio. These investors blindly get attached to their favourite stock and neglect prudent guidelines towards portfolio diversification.

## Diagnostic Testing

These questions are designed to detect cognitive errors stemming from confirmation bias. To complete the test, select the option that best characterises your response to each item.

**Question 1:** Suppose you have invested in a stock for the last five years. Now, you come across a press release that states that the company you have invested in may have a problem with its main product line. However, you also gather information from your friend, who is a long-time investor in the capital market, that the company might be launching a new product in the next two years. How would you deal with such a situation?

a) I will typically take notice of the new product launch and continue my investment without bothering myself with further research.
b) I will typically take notice of the problem with the company's product line and do comprehensive research to decide the next course of action.

**Question 2:** Suppose you have invested in a share for the last ten years and are happy with the investment. The investment appreciates in value but not for the reason you predicted. What is your natural course of action?

a) The company did well. The shares I have selected have generated a profit. This confirms my investment skills and that the stock was a good investment.
b) I am concerned about the investment. I will immediately do further research to find out more information.

**Test Results Analysis**

People who select the option 'a' for both questions are susceptible to bias. In both scenarios, option 'b' is a more rational choice. By answering 'a', the respondent avoids seeking out information that might contradict previously held beliefs regarding the quality of the investment.

## Mitigating Strategies for Confirmation Bias

1. **Be open to all kinds of information and questions:** People should seek out information that could contradict—not just confirm—their investment decisions. It is important to discuss your thoughts openly and invite good questions. The mere existence of contradictory evidence does not necessarily mean an investment is unwise. Rather, uncovering all available data simply facilitates informed decisions. In this context, one should think of adopting strategies like the *six thinking hats* technique which forces moving outside of one's habitual thinking style, looking at things from a number of different perspectives, and having a more rounded view of the situation.
2. **Fundamental research:** Fundamental research on a company, industry, or sector can often provide another informative dimension. This ensures that investment selections do not blindly adhere to preconceived principles while ignoring practical considerations. It is a good idea to document at least one good reason why your final conclusion or view might turn out to be wrong.
3. **Own company bias:** Many employees rationalise their disproportionate investing in the stocks of their companies due to several factors like unique business model, loyalty, familiarity, and optimism.

As high-profile disasters like WorldCom, Enron, and Satyam Computer have shown, employees should follow a structured approach for investing in their own company's stock. In order to guard oneself against confirmation bias, employees should monitor any negative press regarding their own companies, put in place self-imposed investment limits, and regularly research on competing firms and make peer comparison.

4. **Portfolio diversification:** There is a saying 'Don't put all your eggs in one basket' that indicates the benefits of diversification. A well-diversified portfolio not only helps in managing investment risks but also ensures returns over medium to long-term horizon on a sustainable basis. Hence, one should follow portfolio diversification by investing in a range of assets and across several companies.

# 8

# Hindsight Bias

*"Predicting the future is far trickier than most people imagine."*

—Harvard Business Review

Hindsight bias, also referred to as the 'I knew it all along', often occurs in situations where a person believes—after the event—that the occurrence of a past event was predictable and quite obvious, when in fact, the event could not have been reasonably foreseen.

This particular bias leads people to exaggerate the quality of their foresight. Psychologists attribute hindsight bias to our innate need to find order in the world by creating explanations that allow us to believe that events are predictable.

## Example of Hindsight Bias

### Dot-Com Bubble (1995-2000)

The dot-com bubble (also known as tech bubble) was a market stock bubble caused by excessive speculation in Internet-related companies in the late 1990s. There was massive growth in the use and adoption of the Internet between 1995 and its peak in March 2000. The Nasdaq Composite stock market index rose 400% only to fall 78% from its peak by October 2002, giving up most of its gains during the bubble.

Many people claim that the signs of the dot-com bubble were very obvious. This is a clear example of hindsight bias. The important factor to consider here is that if the formation of a bubble had been obvious, it probably would not have risen to the point of bursting. Sadly, even some of the most sophisticated investors succumbed to this fantasy.

**Impact of Hindsight Bias on Investments**

One detriment of hindsight bias is that it can prevent people learning from their mistakes and instead leads them to exaggerate the quality of their foresight. It gives investors a false sense of security when making investment decisions. Here below are some common behaviours rooted in hindsight bias that can cause investment mistakes.

1. **Superior predictive powers:** If the investment appreciates in an upward trending market, then it is likely that hindsight-biased investors would rewrite their own memories to portray the positive developments as if they were predictable. Consequently, the hindsight-biased investors begin to believe that they have superior predictive powers and over time, this rationale can inspire excessive risk-taking and loss.

2. **Self-deception:** Hindsight-biased investors block out recollections of prior incorrect forecasts in order to alleviate embarrassment, especially when they are

performing poorly. This form of self-deception, in some ways similar to cognitive dissonance, prevents investors from learning from their mistakes.

3. **Undue praise or criticism:** During a period of poor performance by fund managers, the hindsight-biased investors tend to unduly blame their managers. Looking back at what has occurred in securities markets, these investors perceive every development as inevitable. In fact, even top-quartile managers who implement their strategies correctly may not succeed in every market cycle. Similarly, hindsight bias can also lead investors to unduly praise their portfolio managers when funds perform well. One should always keep in mind that there are times when portfolio managers benefit from favourable market movements.

## Diagnostic Testing

These questions are designed to detect cognitive errors caused by hindsight bias. To complete the test, select the option that best characterises your response.

**Question 1:** You have invested in a security and it increases in value. However, the underlying reasons for your decisions are not reflected in the current price rise. How do you respond to such a situation?

a) I will do serious research to find out more for my own learning.

b) I will try to understand the underlying reasons for price rise and be careful in future.

c) I will be happy with price appreciation and the fact that I did a great investment. Thus, I can more confidently invest in future.

**Question 2:** You have invested in a security and its price goes down. How do you respond to such a situation?

a) I will do research to find out more for my own learning.
b) I will try to understand the underlying reasons for fall in price and be careful in future.
c) This may be due to bad luck. I will sell the stock and move on, rather than doing further research.

**Question 3:** Suppose you are looking to hire a money manager for your portfolio. Your advisor suggests a large-cap value manager for you. What is your natural approach for examining the manager's performance?

a) I tend to look primarily at a manager's past performance and compare it with a relevant benchmark. I do not concern myself with the strategy that the manager employs.
b) The results that a manager achieves are most important. If returns are good, then I will select that manager. Otherwise, I will look for some other manager.
c) I look at the returns, but I also look at the manager's strategy. I will do an attribution analysis to find out

the manager's own contribution towards the fund performance.

**Test Results Analysis**

Hindsight bias is rather a difficult bias to measure because people are rarely aware that they harbour it. For questions 1 and 2, respondents identifying with the rationale in option 'c' and in question 3, investors answering either 'a' or 'b' are susceptible to hindsight bias.

**Mitigating Strategies for Hindsight Bias**

Giving in to hindsight bias can be very destructive because it leads investors to believe that they have better predictive powers than they actually do. In order to overcome hindsight bias, it is necessary for the investors to understand and admit their susceptibility. Below are some suggested strategies to deal with hindsight bias.

1. **Predicting gains:** When an investor overestimates the degree to which some positive investment outcome was foreseeable, he is susceptible to hindsight bias. He should remind himself that no one can predict the future.
2. **Predicting losses:** When markets go down, many investors prefer to block recollections of poor investment decisions. Understanding why investments go up or down is critical to obtaining insight into markets and finding investment success. One should counsel clients to objectively examine their investment decisions, both good and bad.

This will help eliminate repeats of past investment mistakes.

3. **Avoid undue criticism in the case of poor fund performance:** Clients need to understand the dynamics of economic cycles and markets movements. There are periods when an investment manager will underperform in his or her asset class, relative to other asset classes. Investors should understand that a good manager adheres to a consistent and valid style, through good times and bad. Thus, client education is important to overcome hindsight bias.
4. **Avoid excessive praise in the case of good fund performance:** Using the same line of reasoning, the clients should be counselled against unduly praising a good performance. There are a large number of investment managers who benefit from favourable market cycles and still do not meet benchmarks. Obviously, these are the managers to avoid. Investors should learn how to analyse data and fund performance (attribution analysis). This will help in making the right manager selection and thus, minimise the negative impact of hindsight bias.

# 9

# Illusion of Control Bias

*"One of the hardest things to imagine is that you are smarter than average."*
—Daniel Kahneman

The outcome of every toss of a coin and every spin of the roulette wheel is independent of the previous outcome, making it completely random and a gamble. Stock markets movements often exhibit similar random and unpredictable properties with some difference, i.e., claim on the equity or future earnings. The risk-takers in both gambling and the stock market believe that they can control random or unforeseen events. Illusion of control bias refers to this tendency of humans to overestimate their ability to control events.

**Example of Illusion of Control Bias**

Today is the third India Australia T-20 cricket match. In the last two matches, Australia won the toss. What is the probability of India winning the toss today?

1. Option 1: Australia will win the toss as they have won the toss the last two times.
2. Option 2: India will win this time as they lost the last two times.

Research analysis shows that in the above example, the objective probability is 50 per cent. However, people might judge their subjective probabilities of success higher than the objective probability.

### Impact of Illusion of Control Bias on Investments

1. It is observed from research that traders believe to possess more control over the outcomes of their investments. Such illusion leads investors to trade more, eventually resulting in lower portfolio performance.
2. Another pitfall of control bias is under-diversified portfolios. Researchers have found that many investors end up with concentrated positions because they acquire stocks of companies they feel has some predictability in terms of their performance. However, this control proves to be illusory, and the lack of diversification hurts investors' portfolios.
3. Sometimes, the use of strategies on 'limit orders on buying' or 'cut-loss limits on selling' might provide a false sense of control over portfolio. This might lead to excessive trading and thus may adversely impact portfolio performance.
4. In general, control bias contributes to investors' overconfidence. As a result, investors unknowingly assume more risk than they would normally tolerate.

### Diagnostic Testing

These questions are designed to detect cognitive errors stemming from control bias. To complete the test, select the option that best characterises your response to each item.

**Question 1:** During the last year, your portfolio has done well and beaten the benchmark by 2 per cent. To what do you mainly attribute this positive outcome?

a) My better control of the portfolio.
b) Some combination of investment control and random chance.
c) Completely random chance.

**Question 2:** Suppose you are playing cards. Are you usually more optimistic about the outcome of a hand that you have dealt yourself?

a) Yes. A better outcome will occur when I am controlling the dealing of the cards.
b) No. It makes no difference to me who deals the cards.

**Question 3:** Suppose, you are purchasing a lottery ticket. Do you feel more encouraged regarding your odds of winning, if you choose the number yourself rather than someone else selecting the ticket number?

a) Yes, I am more likely to win if I control the numbers picked.
b) No. It makes no difference to me who chooses the numbers.

**Test Results Analysis**

For the above 3 questions, people responding with option 'a' are susceptible to control bias.

**Mitigating Strategies for Illusion of Control Bias**

A few strategies to mitigate the detrimental financial effects of illusions of control are as follows:

1. **Awareness regarding control bias:** Be aware that investing is a complex process and even the wisest investors have absolutely no control over the outcomes of the investments that they make.
2. **Seek contrary viewpoints:** As you contemplate a new investment, take a moment to ponder whatever considerations might weigh against the trade. Challenge yourself with questions like:

    - Why am I making this investment?
    - What are the downside risks?
    - When will I sell?
    - What might go wrong?

    These important questions can help you to validate your logic behind a decision before implementing that decision.

3. **Maintain records:** Once you have decided to move forward with an investment, one of the best ways to

keep track of the illusion of control is to maintain records of your transactions, including the rationale behind each investment and all important attributes that you have determined to be in favour of the investment's success. Such detailed information will help in periodical reviews and feedback on investment performance.

# 10

# Mental Accounting Bias

*"Money is fungible, but people put it in different mental accounts."*
—Anonymous

One often hears the proverb, "What is mind? It does not matter. What is matter? Never mind." Looking from a behavioural finance standpoint, it matters when we speak of the role played by the mind in managing one's money. Mental accounting is a cognitive bias that describes how people place different values on money based on some subjective criteria. This concept was first named in 1999 by Nobel Prize-winning economist, Richard Thaler, and it elucidates that the individuals classify their money either based on the nature of how it was obtained (salary, inheritance, bonus, lottery, etc.) or the nature of its intended use (child's education, rent, travel, retirement, new house, etc.).

People approach investments in a pyramidical structure. They target low-risk investments for preserving wealth, like cash and money market funds. For income, they rely mostly on bonds and dividend-paying stocks. For creating and multiplying wealth, investors turn to riskier instruments such as emerging market stocks and high coupon bonds.

Combining different assets whose performances do not correlate with one another is an important consideration for risk reduction, but it is often neglected in this pyramid approach. As a result, investment positions held without regard to correlations in a portfolio context creates suboptimal portfolios.

### Example of Mental Accounting Bias

Mr X proposes to buy an apartment. He sets aside funds in a savings bank account. He expects to build a minimum corpus of 20 per cent of the total cost in about one year. Then he wants to buy the apartment by securing a bank home loan for the remaining 80 per cent. His funds in a savings bank account earn an interest @ 3 per cent per annum. He currently also has a credit card loan from the same bank, where he pays interest @ 24 per cent per annum. Mr X has the option of diverting funds from savings bank account to credit card loan and thus save interest to the tune of 21 per cent (24 minus 3). However, Mr X treats the money in the savings bank account and credit card loan differently as these are set for two separate goals.

From an investment perspective, assuming both savings bank and credit card loan run for the next year, Mr X's overall wealth will decrease by an amount of the excess interest (21 per cent) on the credit card loan.

### Impact of Mental Accounting Bias on Investments

Mental accounting is a deep-seated bias. It can cause a variety of problems for investors. The most basic of these problems is the placement of investment assets into discrete 'buckets' without having regard for potential correlations across categories of investments. A few common investment mistakes that mental accounting bias can cause include:

1. **Correlation benefits ignored:** Structuring portfolios in layers to meet different priority goals (buckets) and ignoring correlation across accounts can lead to suboptimal portfolio performance.
2. **Portfolio perspective ignored:** Segregating return into arbitrary categories of income, realised gains, unrealised gains, losses, etc. tends to overemphasise income-generating assets and thereby resulting in a lower total return.
3. **Concentration of company stock:** Mental accounting bias can cause concentration of company stocks, resulting in under-diversified and/or suboptimal portfolios.
4. **House money effect:** Mental accounting bias can cause investors to succumb to what is popularly known as *the house money effect*, wherein the risk-taking behaviour escalates when the wealth grows. Investors behave irrationally because they fail to treat all money as fungible.
5. **Clinging to old profitable portfolios:** People susceptible to mental accounting bias hesitate to sell investments that once generated significant gains but, over time, have fallen in price. This is because of the strong emotional attachment the investors have with the original investments.

## Diagnostic Testing

The following questions are designed to detect signs of mental accounting bias. To complete the test, select the option that best characterises your response to each item.

**Question 1:** Suppose you own two stocks—one with accumulated gain (+ 200 %) and the other trading much below the purchase price (-20%). You need funds urgently and must sell one of the stocks. What will you do?

a) Sell the one with gain and book 200% gain.

b) Sell the one trading below the purchase price and realise the 20% loss.

**Question 2 (a):** Suppose that you have purchased a ticket for your favourite movie. You arrive at the cinema hall excited, but quickly panic as you realise that you have misplaced your ticket! You paid INR 200 for the ticket initially and discover that some similar seats are still available at the same price. What is the probability that you will purchase another INR 200 ticket in order to see the show?

a) 100 per cent.

b) 50 per cent.

c) 0 per cent.

**Question 2 (b):** Suppose that you have not purchased any cinema ticket in advance and plan to buy one for INR 200 at the door. When you arrive at the box office to buy the ticket, you panic because you discover you lost INR 200 while travelling in the local train. There is an ATM close by, so you can still get cash and purchase the ticket. What is the probability that you make a cash withdrawal and then purchase a ticket for INR 200 to see the cinema show?

a) 100 per cent.

b) 50 per cent.

c) 0 per cent.

## Test Result Analysis

### Question 1:

Those who answer 'a' are likely susceptible to mental accounting bias. In this scenario, mental accounting is biased toward selling the winner, even though selling the loser is usually the rational decision due to capital loss tax benefits as well as the fact that the losing stock is a weaker investment. The pain of realising a loss is too much for the investor to bear and so the investor sells the winner to avoid that pain.

### Question 2 (a) and (b):

In the first scenario [Question 2(a)], mental accounting causes people to perceive an aggregate cost of INR 400—the cost of two tickets each costing INR 200. Conversely, for most people, the loss of INR 200 cash and the additional INR 200 ticket are somehow separate in the second scenario [Question 2(b)]. Mentally, these sums are debited from two independent categories or accounts. But in both cases, the total cost comes out to be INR 400. If the respondent indicated a greater willingness to pay for a ticket in part (b) than in part (a), then mental accounting bias is likely present.

**Mitigating Strategies for Mental Accounting Bias**

Mental accounting bias is a common cognitive bias. Nearly everyone is susceptible to this bias in some way or the other. Given below are a few strategies to mitigate mental accounting bias.

1. Individuals should treat money as perfectly fungible when they allocate it among different accounts, be it a budget account (everyday living expenses), a discretionary spending account, or a wealth account (savings and investments).
2. Be aware of the pitfalls of bucket view and benefits of correlations effect in a portfolio view.
3. Review and rebalance portfolio at regular intervals to overcome holding on to losing investments due to emotional reasons.
4. Be aware of excessive concentration in any stock (for example, in your own company stock) and rebalance towards a balanced and diversified portfolio.
5. Sometimes, it is recommended to hold separate investments as a part of 'goals-based planning'. Under such a situation, the risk of not achieving those goals should be effectively monitored and timely remedial measures should be adopted.

# 11

# Recency Bias

*"Today's opinion will make today's prices; tomorrow's opinion tomorrow's prices."*
—Anonymous

Recency bias is the tendency to overweigh the most recent information available to people because such information is fresh in the mind. This cognitive error skews perception towards short-term thinking and affects a lot of traders and investors.

The recency bias, in conjunction with the anchoring bias, creates false intuition regarding market trajectories and leads to skewed calculations. It generally occurs when more recent events play a prominent role in decision-making as compared to events that occurred in the distant past.

**Example of Recency Bias**

1. **Global Financial Crisis (2008)**

   Easy availability of credit in the USA, fueled by large inflows of foreign funds, led to a housing construction boom during 2003-2006. Lax lending standards (banks were lending up to 100% property value) and rising real estate prices attracted hordes of borrowers, including sub-prime ones, to borrow, buy, and make a profit from rising property prices. Loans of various types (mortgage, credit card, auto, etc.) were easy to obtain and consumers assumed an unprecedented debt load expecting the boom will continue (recency bias).

The housing market created an asset bubble in 2006. The falling prices in late 2006 and thereafter resulted in homes worth less than the mortgage loan. The borrowers had little incentive to continue paying a loan collateralised with a home with mostly negative net value and hence, there was widespread foreclosure. The ongoing foreclosure epidemic that began in late 2006 in the USA drained significant wealth from consumers, losing up to $4.2 trillion in wealth from home equity.

**2. Indian Stock Market Boom (2003-07)**

Indian economy witnessed close to a 9% average annual growth rate during 2003-08—one of the world's highest during this period. The spectacular growth was supported by a cyclical credit boom and a surge in foreign capital inflows. The NIFTY index rose from around 1,100 as of March 31, 2002, to a high of 6,000 at the end of December 2007 and thus posting a handsome CAGR return of 40% during a five-year period.

Many first-time retail investors got enchanted by the ongoing bull run and entered the stock market during the peak of 2007. Indian equity market crashed 52% in 2008, in line with the global financial crisis. The investors who entered into the stock market at the fag-end of the bull run in 2007 (recency effect) and exited the next year, amidst a downtrend, incurred huge losses.

**Impact of Recency Bias on Investments**

Investors who suffer from recency bias tend to overvalue the most recent information over historical trends. They may land up in buying stocks which have witnessed sharp price rise recently. Such stocks may be approaching peak valuation. This exposes the investor to avoidable investment loss due to future price correction.

1. Recency bias can cause investors to decide with insufficient historical data and buy assets at the wrong times which, in turn, can lead to losses.
2. Lack of fundamental valuation and only deciding on the recent price pattern exposes the investor to a high risk of loss in case of the market going down. In fact, ignoring the market fundamental and acting only on recent short-term price trend results in market bubbles.
3. Recency bias can cause investors to become addicted to a favourite asset class based on recent market performance and thus exposing the portfolio to high concentration risk.

**Diagnostic Testing**

These questions are designed to detect cognitive errors stemming from recency bias. To complete the test, select the option that best characterises your response to each item.

**Question 1:** Suppose you are asked to select a mutual fund for your portfolio based only on the fund's performance. What is your most likely course of action?

a) I will look at the one to two year record of the fund to see how the fund has done recently.
b) I will look at the five-year track record of the fund, as this time period showcases some elements of recent performance but also historical performance.
c) I will look at the ten-year track record, even though it does not focus on the fund's most recent performance.

**Question 2:** Read the following list of names to the respondents. Then ask, "Did the list contain more male or female names?"

| | |
|---|---|
| • Reeta | • Anand |
| • Steven | • Kavita |
| • Nargis | • Pankaj |
| • Lucy | • Santosh |
| • Sita | • Ram |
| • Mamta | • Shantanu |

**Test Results Analysis**

For Question 1, people who selected response 'a' or 'b' are likely susceptible to recency bias.

The list given in Question 2 actually contains an equal number of male and female names. The male names, however, are concentrated towards the end of the list. Therefore, people who suffer from recency bias are more likely to recall that the list was dominated by male names.

## Mitigating Strategies for Recency Bias

Here below are a few strategies to mitigate/manage the negative impacts of recency bias:

1. **Acknowledge bias:** Half the battle is won with the awareness that the recency bias indeed exists.
2. **Research and analyse:** Recency bias causes investors to place too much emphasis on the data recently gathered. Investors should examine entire relevant bodies of information across extensive time intervals. A top-down and bottom-up analysis made from a deep and wide database should provide relevant information regarding the underlying value of the asset. This valuation should guide the investment decision rather than the recent market performance.
3. **Diversified portfolio:** Investors should avoid portfolio concentration in one or two stocks based on recent performance. Rather, they should focus on strategic asset allocation and portfolio diversification which is essential for long-term investment success.

4. **Financial advisor:** The services of a financial advisor are essential to help the investor in moderating recency bias and constructing a balanced portfolio without being swayed by recency bias.

# 12
# Cognitive Dissonance Bias

*"An investor's worst enemy is not the stock market, but his own emotions."*
—Benjamin Graham

The study of cognitive dissonance is one of the most prominent fields in social psychology. Cognitions, in psychology, represents attitudes, emotions, beliefs, or values. Cognitive dissonance occurs when newly acquired information conflicts with pre-existing understandings, leading to investor's psychological discomfort, irrational decision-making, and investment losses.

In choosing between alternatives, there are sometimes conflict in the decision-making process due to cognitive dissonance bias. Theorists have identified two different aspects of such cognitive dissonance:

1. **Selective perception:** People suffering from selective perception only register information that appears to affirm a chosen course. It produces a view or understanding that could be incomplete and inaccurate. And this lack of complete or objective understanding of available evidence leads to miscalculations.

2. **Selective decision-making:** Selective decision-making usually occurs when the commitment to an original decision course is high. Selective decision-making rationalises actions that enable a person to adhere to that course, even if at an exorbitant economic cost.

**Examples of Cognitive Dissonance**

1. You are a conservationist and believe that humans need to protect the environment. However, you still use plastic garbage bags. That feeling of mental discomfort about using plastic bags is an example of cognitive dissonance. This is because your beliefs are clashing with your actions or behaviour.
2. Let us assume that ABC is looking to buy a stock of an XYZ limited. He believes that XYZ will perform well in the future. XYZ limited stock is currently trading in the market at INR 450 and ABC is thinking to buy the stock if it falls below INR 400. In three days, the stock price hit INR 418. ABC thinks the stock price will soon come down to INR 400. However, after another three days, suddenly the stock price goes up and reaches INR 500 because of buying demand from other investors. In such a scenario, ABC will probably experience cognitive dissonance. He may think that the stock was good at INR 418 and that he missed an opportunity. There are high chances that ABC will buy some XYZ stock at INR 500 to relieve the discomfort he feels. He may also rationalise his decision by thinking that buying an

XYZ stock at a higher price is still good because other investors are also buying at the same price.

3. Suppose that ABC bought a stock of MNP limited at a price of INR 800. In the next week, the stock price of MNP fell and upon analysis, ABC came to know that MNP's aggressive inorganic growth has filled their balance sheet with debt. By this time, the stock was trading at INR 600. ABC bought some more stock again. His understanding was that the company made good quality products and he read the report that once the economic condition improves and interest rates come down, company stock will perform well. ABC was buying at every fall in stock price while looking for some good news about the company to support his buying decision at every fall. Despite successive falls, ABC still hopes that the company's position will improve, and he will get the stock price of INR 800 at least.

**Impact of Cognitive Dissonance Bias on Investments**

1. When it comes to investing, cognitive dissonance bias can cause investors to fail in making good investment decisions as it usually leads to holding losing investments because they want to avoid the mental pain associated with admitting that they have made a poor decision.
2. Sometimes, cognitive dissonance bias can cause investors to continue to invest in a security that they already own after it has gone down in order to confirm an earlier decision to invest in that security, without judging the rationality of such a strategy.

3. Cognitive dissonance bias can cause investors to get caught up in irrational decision-making. They avoid information that counters an earlier decision (cognitive dissonance).
4. Cognitive dissonance bias causes investors to believe the concept 'It's different this time'. People who purchase stocks at the height of bull-run ignore the evidence that they are purchasing the most expensive stocks and assuming excessive risks.

**Diagnostic Testing**

This test showcases a scenario that illustrates susceptibility to cognitive dissonance bias. To complete the test, select the option that best characterises your response to the question given below.

**Question 1:** Suppose that you recently bought a new car. You are happy with the purchase. Soon after your purchase, you discover that another car is giving an additional five-year free motor insurance package with the car. What is your likely reaction in such as case:

a) You immediately research some consumer magazines to find out more information about the current trends in discounts and free gifts.
b) You contact your car dealer to ascertain if you missed a significant opportunity.
c) The prospect of discovering an error in your purchase makes you uncomfortable. Hence, you decide to enjoy the car without any further research.

**Test Result Analysis**

For the above question, people responding with option 'c' indicate a propensity for cognitive dissonance bias.

**Common Coping Tendencies for Cognitive Dissonance Bias**

When there are conflicts between cognitions (thoughts, beliefs, opinions, etc.), people take steps to reduce the dissonance and feelings of discomfort. Looking from the perspective of personal finance and investments, Michael M. Pompian, author of *Behavioural Finance and Wealth Management*, mentions three common approaches to cognitive dissonance (all with negative implications for investments) as noted below:

1. **Modifying beliefs:** Perhaps this is the easiest way to manage cognitive dissonance. People can try to resolve dissonance between actions and beliefs by altering relevant beliefs. For example, if the behaviour in question was 'selling a losing investment', one might concoct some rationale along the lines of 'it is okay not to sell a losing investment' in order to resolve cognitive dissonance and then hold onto a stock. Such behaviour, obviously, can pose serious hazards to one's wealth.

2. **Modifying actions:** On realising that they have engaged in behaviour contradictory to some pre-existing belief, people might condition themselves against committing a similar action in the future. The dissonance associated with having violated a basic precept of investment strategy dissipates.

3. **Modifying perceptions of relevant action(s):** A more difficult approach is to rationalise the conflicting action with the beliefs. For example, an investor might rationalise a losing investment with a justification like 'I don't really need the money right now, so I won't sell'. However, it is a harmful attitude and must be avoided.

**Mitigating Strategies for Cognitive Dissonance Bias**

1. **Recognition of cognitive dissonance bias:** The first step in overcoming the negative effects of cognitive dissonance is to recognise that a faulty cognition has occurred. In case of a poor investment made in the past, investors should objectively analyse the underlying issues and identify the relevant biases, if any, for appropriate remedial action.
2. **Education on behavioural finance:** Investors and other market participants need to educate themselves on behavioural biases in general and their cognitive dissonance in particular, the ways to modify their own behaviours, and how to separate biases from the investment decision-making process.
3. **Rational action for balanced portfolio:** Having identified the problem, i.e., self-discovery of cognitive dissonance, and educating oneself on how to separate irrational biases from the investment decision-making process, it is time to take rational actions required for modifying existing portfolio towards strategic asset allocation and diversifying portfolio keeping with long-term financial goals.

The behavioural transformation described above is rather complex but in the long run, this will likely help the market practitioner evolving into a much better investor.

13

# Endowment Bias

*"Look at the market fluctuations as your friend rather than your enemy."*

—Warren Buffet

Endowment bias is an emotional bias that leads people to place a higher value on an asset that they already own compared to others ones they do not. As per the standard economic theory, under normal circumstances, a person's willingness to pay for an asset (buy) should always be equal to the person's willingness to part with the same asset (sell). However, psychologists have found that this equation does not always hold good. There are situations when the minimum selling price that the people state to part the asset tend to be much higher than the maximum purchase price that they are willing to pay for the same asset. This mental process, in which a differential weight is placed on the same asset, is popularly known as endowment bias.

Endowment bias could be traced to two main psychological thinking:

1. **Ownership:** Things are valued more preciously by those who already own them (example, property right) than by those who wish to get them.

2. **Loss Aversion:** Human beings are more prone towards loss-aversion and there is a feeling of loss (opportunity loss) from forgoing the object.

**Example of Endowment Bias**

One of the best examples of the endowment effect is a study by Daniel Kahneman and others in which participants were given a mug and then offered the chance to sell it or trade it for an equally valued alternative (pens). They found that the amount participants required as compensation for the mug once their ownership of the mug had been established (willingness to accept) was approximately twice as high as the amount they were willing to pay to acquire the mug (willingness to pay).

**Impact of Endowment Bias on Investments**

Generally, endowment bias negatively impacts investment performance in the following major areas:

1. **Inherited securities:** People who inherit shares of stock from deceased relatives exhibit the endowment effect by refusing to divest those shares, even if they do not fit with that individual's risk tolerance or investment goals. This could be either due to the loyalty effect, tax consequences, or transaction cost. Such failure to sell off certain assets and replace them with other more profitable assets may negatively impact diversification and result in suboptimal portfolios.
2. **Purchased securities:** Similarly, endowment bias causes investors to hold securities they have purchased or already own. At times, such biased

behaviour places an irrational premium on the compensation demanded in exchange for parting with an endowed asset.

3. **Transaction cost:** Endowment bias causes investors to hold securities that they have either inherited or purchased because they do not want to incur the transaction costs associated with churning the portfolio. These costs, however, can be a very small price to pay when selling inappropriate investments in favour of a more profitable portfolio aligned with the investor's financial goals and risk tolerance.
4. **Familiarity:** Endowment bias causes investors to hold poorly performing securities that they have either inherited or purchased because they are familiar with the behavioural characteristics of these legacy investments. Familiarity adds to owners' perceived value of a security.

## Diagnostic Testing

These questions are designed to detect cognitive errors stemming from endowment bias. To complete the test, select the option that best characterises your response to each item.

**Question 1:** Assume that your affectionate grandfather used to work for Hindustan Unilever Limited (HUL). He had bequeathed to you 2,000 shares of Hindustan Unilever. Your financial advisor tells you that your portfolio has too much concentration risk and recommends that you sell HUL shares. What is your most likely course of action?

a) I will likely hold the HUL shares because my sweet grandfather bequeathed these stocks to me.

b) I will likely listen to my financial advisor and sell the shares.

**Question 2:** Assume that you have purchased a high-quality infrastructure bond for your portfolio and it has been providing income for you and you are happy with it. Your financial advisor analyses your bond holdings and recommends switching to a AAA-rated corporate bond of comparable quality and 50 basis points higher return. What is your most likely response?

a) I will stick with the infrastructure bond because I am familiar with it.

b) I will sell the infrastructure bond and purchase the corporate bond, even though I am unfamiliar with the corporate bond.

**Question 3:** Assume that you have purchased 1000 shares of Nestle in a self-directed account and paid a commission on the transaction. Shortly following the purchase, you realise that you momentarily overlooked another 1000 shares of Nestle that you already owned in another account. Nestle now constitute 80% of your portfolio. Now, the excessive holdings are causing an imbalance in your overall portfolio. What is your reaction to this situation?

a) Since I paid a commission and I like Nestle stock, I will keep Nestle even though it may cause an imbalance in my overall portfolio.

b) I am not comfortable with an imbalance in my portfolio. I will sell Nestle, even though this means that I will have paid two commissions.

**Test Results Analysis**

Question 1: A reluctance to offload HUL shares can signal susceptibility to endowment bias.

Question 2: People who decide that they might likely hold onto the infrastructure bond, due to familiarity with it, are likely to exhibit endowment bias than people who would be willing to reallocate for AAA corporate bond at a financial advisor's request, even though it is unfamiliar territory.

Question 3: Respondents who estimate that they would be willing to tolerate the imbalance caused by the excessive Nestle holdings are probably susceptible to endowment bias.

**Mitigating Strategies for Endowment Bias**

The endowment effect refers to an emotional bias that causes individuals to value an owned object higher, often irrationally, than its market value. From a portfolio management perspective, below are a few suggested strategies to mitigate the negative impacts of endowment bias:

1. **Inherited securities:** Understanding the origins of endowment bias can provide some insights in addressing mitigating solutions. Often, challenging the existing portfolio with a few carefully targeted

questions is a useful first step. This way, one can lead clients to discover the correct conclusion themselves. For example, one might ask: "If you had received cash instead of this security, what portion of that inheritance would you allocate into this specific security?" Often, the answer is none or very little. It can also be useful to explore the deceased's intent in owning the security. "Do you think that grandfather's primary intent was to leave you this specific number of shares of this specific security? And is it possible that he was concerned about your general financial security?" Such probing questions may enable the clients to understand the benefits of a more sensible allocation towards a diversified portfolio.

2. **Purchased securities:** Regular review and rebalancing of existing portfolio should be done to identify stocks reaching peak valuations or stocks with deteriorating fundamentals. If need be, the owned stocks should be sold and replaced with stocks of more reasonable valuation. The question to ask is: "Would you buy the same stock/portfolio if you are given cash today?" If the answer is no, then the better option would be portfolio rebalancing.
3. **Transaction cost:** Very often, the aversion to commission can be very harmful to one's portfolio. One should examine whether avoidance of portfolio rebalancing is merely due to such 'penny wise, pound foolish' principle. If yes, then the best way is to numerically demonstrate the potential gains that can be achieved or losses that can be avoided

by selling versus retaining the security. Once facts about the benefits of higher potential return from the rebalanced portfolio are presented, the clients are likely to understand the benefits and agree to replace the existing securities.

4. **Familiarity:** Familiarity assumes special significance and can be difficult to overcome. An effective way to address this pitfall is to review the historical performance of the unfamiliar (proposed) securities that are being suggested to the client. Demonstrating the logic underlying the recommendation rather than entirely replacing familiar holdings is a preferred approach. Rather than replacing all familiar holdings with the new, intimidating ones, it is imperative to start with a small purchase of the unfamiliar investments until a comfort level with them is achieved. This way, the client can develop familiarity with the new investments and rebalance the portfolio with appropriate asset allocation in a phased manner.

# 14

# Self-Attribution (Self-Serving) Bias

*"People come to the stock market with lots of money and zero experience. They leave the market with lots of experience and zero money."*
—Anonymous

Self-attribution bias, also known as self-serving bias, refers to the tendency of individuals to attribute successes (good outcomes) to their own talent, skills, research, and foresight, while blaming failures (bad outcomes) on outside factors or bad luck. The bias is widely observed across populations even though it varies by age, geographies, and culture.

Self-attribution bias can be technically broken down into two subcomponents:

i. **Self-enhancing bias** refers to one's propensity to irrationally claim credit for success.

ii. **Self-protecting bias** represents the irrational denial of responsibility for failure.

**Examples of Self-Attribution Bias**

1. A student often attributes earning a good grade on an examination to his/her own intelligence and preparation but attributes a poor grade to the teacher's poor teaching ability or unfair test questions.
2. A job applicant believes that he has been hired because of his superior talent, qualifications, or excellent interview. In case of failure to receive an offer, he/she may blame the interviewer as biased.
3. An investor purchases an investment and it goes up. The investor thinks it was due to specialised skills. In contrast, when it goes down, then it is viewed to be due to bad luck or some other factor and not as the fault of the investor.

**Impact of Self-Attribution Bias on Investments**

The self-attribution bias impairs investors in two different ways. First, people who cannot identify their mistakes fail to learn from those mistakes. Second, investors who irrationally credit themselves for good outcomes can become overconfident in their trading and investment decisions. Given below are a few examples of self-attribution bias negatively impacting investments:

1. Self-attribution investors irrationally attribute investment success to their own expertise rather than to factors out of their control. This behaviour can lead to taking on too much risk as the investors become overconfident.

2. Self-attribution bias often leads investors to indulge in excessive trading. This leads to higher trading expenses and portfolio underperformance.
3. Self-attribution bias leads investors to a situation where investors only like to hear success stories. Whenever some positive investment outcome is presented, then they ascribe this brilliance to themselves. Such an attitude may lead the investors to purchase and hold under-performing investments for a long duration.
4. Self-attribution bias can cause investors to hold under-diversified portfolios. This phenomenon is more prevalent among investors who attribute the success of a company's performance to their own contribution. Consequently, this may result in investors holding on to a concentrated stock position.

## Diagnostic Testing

**Question 1:** You purchase an IT stock. Soon after your purchase, you overhear a news item that has negative implications on the investment you have just made. How likely are you to seek new information that could confirm that you have made a poor decision?

a) Very unlikely.
b) Unlikely.
c) Likely.
d) Very likely.

**Question 2:** The returns on your portfolio for the last one year is higher than the market benchmark. You believe that the better portfolio performance is primarily due to:

a) Your investment skill.

b) A combination of investment skill and luck.

c) Luck.

**Question 3:** You have just booked profit from a successful trade. How likely you are to put your profits to work?

a) When I sell a profitable investment, I usually invest the money again right away.

b) I will usually wait until I find some other good investment.

c) Some combination of choices 'a' and 'b'.

**Question 4:** How do you rate yourself when compared to other investors?

a) Below average.

b) Average.

c) Above average.

d) Well above average.

**Test Results Analysis**

Question 1: People whose response indicates that they would be unlikely to seek information that could implicate them in a previous poor decision are likely to suffer from self-attribution bias. This is so because an investment failure is perceived to be due to bad luck and not due to poor decision-making.

Question 2: Attributing financial success to one's own investment skill indicates tendency towards self-attribution bias.

Question 3: Investors who roll over their money immediately without carefully researching the next investment idea are irrationally attributing their successes to their own skills and competence. They are likely to suffer from self-attribution bias.

Question 4: Investors who rate themselves as 'above average' or 'well above average' in skill are likely to suffer from self-attribution bias.

## Mitigating Strategy for Self-Attribution Bias

1. One of the best tools to overcome self-attribution bias is to carry out post-investment analysis to identify good investment decisions (money made) from bad ones (money lost). Further analysis will show how much of the success or failure can be attributed to market movement rather than the skill of the investor.

2. Investors should do research into poor decisions to find out what went wrong. Questions like the ones given below can throw insights into the causes of unprofitable trades.

    - Did you buy stocks with poor earnings?

- Were those stocks trading at or near their recent price highs when you purchased them?
- Did you pick up the stocks as they were beginning to decline?
- Was the market, in general, undergoing a correction phase?

3. When reviewing unprofitable decisions, look for patterns or common mistakes that perhaps you were unaware of at the time of executing the trade. Such a review will help you overcome any bad habits that you may have acquired and can also reinforce your reliance on the strategies that have served you well.
4. Regular review and monitoring of portfolio and learning from past mistakes is the best way to overcome self-attribution bias and emerge as a successful investor in the long run.

# 15

# Regret Aversion Bias

*"Nobody has ever bet enough on the winning horse."*

—Richard Sasuly

Regret aversion, an emotional bias, seeks to avoid the emotional pain of regret associated with poor decision-making. People who are susceptible to this bias try to avoid distress arising from errors of omission (example, not buying the right investment or property) and errors of commission (example, buying the wrong investment or property).

When people fear that their decision will turn out to be wrong in hindsight, they exhibit regret aversion bias. It is a cognitive phenomenon that often arises in investors, causing them to hold onto losing positions for too long in order to avoid admitting errors of realising losses. Regret aversion also makes people unduly apprehensive about breaking into financial markets that have recently generated losses. In fact, people suffering from regret aversion bias hesitate most during the period that merits aggressive behaviour.

Regret aversion also affects a person's response to investment gains. People exhibiting regret aversion can be reluctant to book profit from an investment whose value has climbed recently beyond the target price. Regret-averse investors may stick to positions that they ought to sell, pained by the prospect that the investment, if sold, might go up even higher.

**2008 USA Subprime Crisis**

The subprime mortgage crisis in the United States of America between 2007 and 2010 was triggered by a large decline in home prices leading to mortgage delinquencies, foreclosures, and the devaluation of securities related to mortgage finance. The new homebuyers refused to walk away from their mortgages, even though their property values were falling rapidly. Research in 2010 found that property values had to drop below 75% of the outstanding loans before homeowners considered walking away. If decisions had been based solely on rational economic factors, many owners would have walked away sooner. Instead, emotional attachment to the homes, combined with an aversion to regret seeing money previously invested losing value so fast, caused them to delay their decision.

**Examples of Regret Aversion**

Regret aversion may be due to error of omission or error of commission. The following examples illustrate the same:

1. **Error of Omission**

   Govind, a hypothetical investor, had a chance to invest in an initial public offering (IPO) that has generated a great buzz. However, the fear of losing money led to indecision and he missed the deadline for IPO application. The stock appreciates by 40% in three months of the listing in the stock exchange.

Govind has committed an error of omission because he omitted the IPO and lost out.

2. **Error of Commission**

   Siddharth, a hypothetical investor, invested in an upcoming e-commerce company believing that the price will rise but the price of the stock fell by 30% in the six months. He committed an error of commission for not doing enough research and regrets losing the money.

It is pertinent to note that the emotional pain from the error of omission described above may not be as strong as that associated with the error of commission expressed above. This is because, for investors, the hurt that arises from losing money outweighs the joy of gaining money. Also, in the first possibility, the investor merely did not act and only lost out on the opportunity to gain, whereas in the second possibility, the investor committed the act of investing and lost money.

### Impact of Regret Aversion Bias on Investments

Given below are some common investor mistakes associated with the regret aversion bias:

1. **Portfolio underperformance due to investing conservatively:** Regret aversion bias can cause investors to be excessively conservative in their investment choices. Having suffered losses in the past, many people shy away from making new bold investment decisions and accept only low-risk

positions. Such behaviour can lead to long-term underperformance and a failure to meet investment goals.

2. **Staying away from profitable investments in a down-trending market:** Regret aversion bias can cause investors to stay away from markets that have recently gone down. They fear that if they invest, such a market might subsequently continue its downward trend, prompting them to regret the decision to buy in. However, depressed markets offer great bargains. Such market down-trend offers excellent opportunities to invest in the undervalued investments and thereby reap handsome gains when eventually market recovers.
3. **Holding on to losing investments for too long:** Regret aversion can cause investors to hold on to losing positions for too long. People don't like to admit when they are wrong, and they will go to great lengths to avoid selling a losing investment. This behaviour, similar to loss aversion, is hazardous to one's wealth.
4. **Herd behaviour:** This is a form of regret aversion where participants go with the consensus or popular opinion. Essentially, this gives participants psychological comfort as they can tell themselves that they are not to blame if others are wrong as well. However, such behaviour does not help. For example, the demise of the Internet stock bubble demonstrated that even the most massive herd can stampede in the wrong direction.

5. **Preference for good companies:** Regret aversion bias leads investors to prefer stocks of subjectively categorised 'good companies', even when an alternative stock has an equal or a higher expected return. This is because regret-averse investors may feel that the pain from a failure of investments in riskier companies will be dramatically much higher compared to the consequences of investing in a so-called safe stock.
6. **Holding on to winning investments for too long:** Regret aversion can cause investors to hold onto winning stocks for too long. People fear that by selling a stock that has been doing well, they might miss out on further imminent gains.

**Diagnostic Testing**

These questions are designed to detect signs of emotional bias stemming from regret aversion. To complete the test, select the option that best characterises your response to each item.

**Question 1:** Suppose that you make an investment in stock A and over the next 12 months, it appreciates by 10%. You contemplate selling stock A for normal portfolio rebalancing purposes but then come across a positive news item highlighting that stock A could climb even higher. Which answer describes your likeliest response, given A's recent performance and this new information?

a) I think I will hold on to my stock and sell later. I would really regret if I sold now and A continues to go up.

b) I will probably sell. But I will still kick myself if A appreciates later on.

c) I will probably sell the stock without any second thoughts about what happens to A's price after the transaction.

**Question 2:** Suppose that you have decided to acquire 1000 shares of ABC company. You purchase 500 shares at INR 200 apiece and strategise to wait a few days before picking up the additional 500. Further suppose that soon after your initial buy, the market takes a comprehensive dip. ABC is now trading at INR 182, with no change in fundamentals. Which answer most closely matches your thought process in this situation?

a) I will probably wait until the stock begins to go up before buying the remaining 500 shares. I really do not want to see ABC fall below INR 182 because I would regret my initial decision to buy in.

b) I will probably buy the remaining 500 shares. Though, if ABC ends up going below INR 182, I will regret my decision.

c) I will probably buy the remaining 500 shares. Even if ABC falls below INR 182, I don't think that I will experience a lot of regret.

**Question 3:** Suppose you have decided to invest INR 20,000 in the stock market. You have narrowed your choices down to two companies: ABC and XYZ. According to your calculations, both stocks have equal risk and return payoffs. ABC is a well-followed, eminently established company whose shareholders include many large pension funds. XYZ has performed well but has not garnered the same kind of public profile as ABC and only has few well-known investors. Which answer most closely matches your thought process in this situation?

a) I will most likely invest in ABC because I feel safe taking the same course as so many respected institutional investors. If ABC does decline in value, I know I will not be the only one caught by surprise and with so many savvy professions also sharing my predicament, I could hardly blame myself for excessively poor judgement.

b) I will most likely invest in ABC because if I invested in XYZ and my investment failed, I would feel like a fool. Few well-known investors backed XYZ and I would really regret going against their informed consensus only to discover that I was wrong.

c) I would feel indifferent between the two investments since both generated the same expected parameters for risk and return.

**Test Result Analysis**

Questions 1, 2, and 3: People answering 'a' or 'b' to any of the above questions may be susceptible to regret aversion bias.

### Mitigating Strategies for Regret Aversion Bias

Broadly speaking, having a basic understanding of an investor's psychological profile and building an appropriate portfolio consistent with the defined objectives and risk tolerance of the client can limit the negative fallout from regret aversion bias. Here below are a few strategies to address the specific pitfalls of regret aversion.

1. **Investing too conservatively:** It is essential to understand the long-term benefits of adding risky assets to a portfolio for diversification. Efficient frontier research can be very helpful here. Despite possible losses from past investing, the client should learn the benefits of the portfolio approach to achieve future goals. Investors who completely avoid risky assets due to regret aversion bias may see less growth in their portfolios than they could otherwise achieve.
2. **Herd behaviour:** If an individual reflects herd mentality, then it can help to stop and question the investor's motivations. Effective communication about the benefits of diversification, expected asset allocation keeping with the individual risk and return objectives, and the consequences of not meeting critical long-term investment goals will likely help in mitigating regret aversion bias.
3. **Holding losing positions for too long:** While realising losses is never enjoyable, the wisdom here is that following an unprofitable decision, it is best to cut losses and move on. Loss is an unavoidable

part of investment strategy and it is prudent to own one's mistakes when it happens. If people can learn to view the market and portfolios objectively, then the pain of owning up to the loss will be reduced and the regret aversion will be lower.

4. **Preference for good companies:** Investors often think they can save face by buying stock in well-reputed companies. However, such great companies also have their share of ups and downs, just like any other competing firms. Hence, clients should not limit themselves to good companies simply because they fear the regret they might experience if an investment in a lesser-known company does not work out. Remember that high-profile brands do not necessarily deliver good returns.

5. **Holding winners for too long:** The aim of investments is to make a profit. However, if there is a fundamental reason that favours selling a security (example, it is overvalued) and if the only reason not to sell is because of the fear of regretting a missed opportunity should the investment appreciate after one sells it, then it's time to take a step back. One should remember that one can experience regret when a stock begins to decline after reaching a certain level. Moreover, a helpful approach here is to attempt to set aside any emotions that might be impacting the sell decision. It is advisable to have defined limits for 'book profit' and once the price reaches the limit, one should book profit and move on. After all, one can always buy in again later if

the stock does indeed represent a good investment opportunity.

6. **Staying out of the market after a loss:** There is no principle more fundamental in securities trading than *buy low, sell high*. It is human nature to chase returns by following 'hot' money. But the problem here is that one never precisely knows the trends and price movements of individual stocks or markets. Thus, disciplined, prudent and informed decision-making is crucial to long-term success.

# 16

# Status Quo Bias

*"One day everything will be well, that is our hope. Everything is fine today, that is our illusion."*

—Voltaire

Status quo bias, coined by Samuelson and Zeckhauser (1988), is an emotional bias which is characterised by people doing nothing (maintain the 'status quo') instead of making a change. Human habits are often exceptionally strong and difficult to change, and when faced with a choice, people tend to go with the flow of preset options. Given an array of choices with one choice as the default choice, people will likely let that default choice stand rather than making a new choice. In other words, status quo bias operates in people who prefer for things to stay relatively the same.

Status quo bias is often discussed in tandem with other biases, namely endowment bias and loss aversion bias. Status quo bias differs from these two in that it does not depend on framing changes in terms of losses and potential gains. When loss aversion bias and status quo bias cross paths, it is probable that an investor, who has to choose between two investment alternatives, will stick to the status quo if it seems less likely to trigger a loss—even if the status quo also guarantees a lower return in the long run. Endowment bias supports status quo bias, i.e., people don't want to give up their endowments. There is also a likelihood of both loss aversion bias and endowment bias combining with status quo bias resulting in further hardening of the behaviour to keep things to stay as they are, even if it comes at a cost.

### Examples of Status Quo Bias

A few real-world examples of status quo bias are noted below:

1. A new coal-mining project forced the citizens of a town in north Odisha to be relocated to a similar area nearby. They were offered several options by the government. The citizens stayed put in their old place, even though the layout was inefficient and confusing. They refused to move to a better-planned locality with more facilities.
2. When offered several sandwich options for lunch, individuals often choose a sandwich they have eaten before. This phenomenon is called regret avoidance. And in seeking to avoid a potential regrettable experience (choosing a new sandwich and disliking it), individuals opt to stick with the status quo (the sandwich with which they are already familiar).
3. When a company added new insurance plans to the list of insurance options, existing employees chose the old plans much more frequently as compared to new employees. New employees tended to select new plans.

4. Participants in a retirement plan were given the option of changing the distribution of their investments every year at no cost. Yet, despite varying rates of return among different options, only 2.5% of participants changed their distribution in any given year. When asked why they never changed their plan distribution, participants often couldn't justify their preference for the status quo.
5. Investors with inherited, concentrated stock positions often exhibit classic status quo bias. Take the case of a hypothetical grandson who hesitates to sell the bank stock he has inherited from his grandfather. Even though his portfolio is under-diversified and could benefit from such an adjustment, the grandson favours the status quo.
6. Besides loss aversion and endowment biases, several other motives like psychological inertia, fear of regret in making a wrong decision, aversion to tax consequences or any other transaction costs, etc. could be at work in the above examples.

## Impact of Status Quo Bias on Investments

Four common investment mistakes that can arise from status quo bias are described below:

1. Status quo bias can cause investors to stick to portfolios that are inappropriate for their risk-return profile. This could mean that investors continue with existing portfolios, taking no actions and thereby not

being able to take advantage of better investment opportunities available in the market.

2. Status quo bias can combine with loss aversion bias and offers the investor a choice of avoiding booking a loss from rebalancing the legacy portfolio. This will be true even if, in the long run, the investor could achieve a much higher return by electing an alternative portfolio of assets.
3. Status quo bias causes investors to hold poorly performing securities with which they feel familiar or to which they are emotionally attached. Such behaviour can compromise financial goals.
4. Status quo bias can cause investors to hold securities, either inherited or purchased, because of an aversion to tax incidence or other transaction costs associated with selling. This behaviour can be hazardous to one's wealth because such transaction cost or tax effect is normally a small price to pay for exiting the poorly performing investments and building a robust portfolio.

### Diagnostic Testing

The following questions are designed to detect signs of cognitive errors stemming from status quo bias. To complete the test, select the choice that best characterises your response to each item.

**Question 1:** Which of the following would you choose?

a) A 100 per cent chance of winning INR 100,000.

b) An 80 per cent chance of winning INR 132,000 with a 20 per cent chance of winning nothing.

**Question 2:** Your investment portfolio contains a certain high-quality corporate bond. The bond has been providing good income for you, and you are happy with it. Your financial advisor analyses your bond holdings and recommends that you replace the corporate bond with another 20-year bond recently issued by a reputed state government. The new bond is of better credit quality and also provides about 10 basis points higher return. However, you aren't familiar with this new bond issued by the state government. What is your most likely response?

a) I will sell the corporate bond and purchase the state government bond.

b) I will keep things as they are.

**Question 3:** Suppose that you have inherited shares of a gold mining company from your maternal grandfather. After a review of your portfolio, your financial advisor concludes that your portfolio is highly concentrated with gold and commodities stocks. She recommends selling these shares in favour of a diversified portfolio. How would you likely react?

a) Sure, I will sell the shares, as recommended by my financial advisor.

b) No, I will hold onto these shares because I do not like to sell or modify things that people pass away and leave to me.

**Test Result Analysis**

Question 1: This question presents a classic intersection of status quo bias and loss aversion bias. People selecting option 'a' exhibit a little of each. The unbiased option is 'b' which has a higher expected value (INR 105,600) than option 'a'.

Question 2: People who select the option 'b' are likelier to suffer from status quo bias than people who select the option 'a' which offers higher returns.

Question 3: In this situation, most people would generally behave as depicted in option 'b', even when lacking any economic rationale for holding the asset. Thus, option 'b' suggests status quo bias.

**Mitigating Strategies for Status Quo Bias**

Status quo bias may be exceptionally strong and difficult to overcome. Given below are a few strategies to cope with the pitfalls of status quo bias.

1. **Recognising the bias is the first step:** Many experts in behavioural science believe that if we are aware of how our biases affect our everyday lives, we are already halfway to changing our behaviour for the better.

2. **Investment education:** Demonstrating the downside risks associated with holding inappropriate assets (example, a market downturn significantly depleting 70 per cent of wealth level), forces people to accept lifestyle changes. This is often an effective strategy and may motivate people to change their behaviour.
3. **Strategic asset allocation:** Doing nothing is much easier than deciding. However, sometimes inaction can compromise long-run returns. An advisor should quantify the risk-reducing and return-enhancing advantages of proper asset allocation and demonstrate the benefits of decisive action.
4. **Emotional attachment:** Emotions are perhaps the least legitimate concerns in asset management. When financial goals are in jeopardy, it can be too risky to sit back and adhere to an affective whim. Thus, advisors need to demonstrate how emotions need to be managed.
5. **Fear of tax and transaction costs:** Taxes and fees are legitimate concerns when it comes to rebalancing the portfolio. However, such transaction cost or tax effect is normally a small price to pay for exiting the poorly performing investments and building a robust portfolio. The advisor should run through some financial calculations, demonstrate the risk and return profile of both the existing and re-balanced portfolio (proposed), and clearly demonstrate the advantages of a superior diversified portfolio aligned to the client's financial goals.

## 17

# Overconfidence Bias

*"The investor's chief problem—and even his worst enemy—is likely to be himself."*

—Benjamin Graham

Looking from investments and capital market perspective, overconfidence is one of the most common and prolific individual bias. Overconfidence bias occurs when market participants overestimate their own intuitive reasoning, judgements, knowledge, skills, or cognitive abilities. In short, it is about believing that they are smarter in predicting future security price or market movement than they actually are. It is difficult for most individuals to correct overconfidence bias as it is deeply rooted in the desire to feel good about one's decision-making ability. Overconfidence bias can be of two types:

1. **Certainty overconfidence** leads individuals to constantly chase the 'next hot stock'. In such a case, investors generally underestimate uncertainty about their investment prediction. For example, executives of a publicly traded blue-chip company may consider the company as a good investment bet and refuse to diversify their concentrated holding of

the stock. It is well known that many of the highly-rated corporates in the past (Enron, WorldCom, Blockbuster, Swissair, Kingfisher Airlines, Bisleri, Satyam Computers, and IL&FS to name a few) have vanished over years.

2. **Prediction overconfidence** occurs when investors underestimate the downside risks to their forecast of stock price or future index level. The confidence intervals that an investor may assign to their investment predictions usually are too narrow. For example, an investor may forecast the future price of a stock, predicting between 10 per cent gain or decline, but there may be much wider standard deviations.

**Examples of Overconfidence Bias**

1. A person who thinks he has a photographic memory and a detailed understanding of a subject could show his overconfidence by deciding not to study adequately for a test and thus does poorly on the test due to lack of preparation.
2. A person who thinks he is invaluable to his employer when almost anyone could actually do his job might show his overconfidence by coming in late to work or by being overly demanding about getting a raise because he thinks he is never going to get fired.
3. A person who thinks his spouse or partner will never leave because he or she loves him too much. The

person might try to take advantage of the spouse or partner due to this overconfidence and in turn, drive the spouse away.

4. A person who thinks he is the best badminton player and challenges someone who is a world-class badminton player. The person who was overconfident and was mistaken about his actual badminton playing abilities could end up getting badly defeated as a result of his overconfidence.
5. A person, who is convinced that he is going to get into the best school, applies only to the top school. The overconfidence of this person could result in not getting into any school and missing the academic year.
6. A politician, who is self-assured about his win, does not bother to campaign aggressively as a result of his overconfidence. The overconfidence could result in losing the election.

## Impact of Overconfidence Bias on Investments

1. **Overestimating return and underestimating risk:** Overconfident investors overestimate their ability to evaluate a stock as a potential investment. Because of this biased judgement, they may hold on to an investment despite the negative information and warning signs.
2. **Excessive trading:** Overconfidence leads to excessive trading because the practitioners believe that they have special knowledge which others do not have.

Excessive trading raises transaction costs and leads to lower portfolio performance.

3. **Portfolio underperformance:** There is a fair amount of research pointing to the fact that overconfident investors do not heed to performance results and tend to continuously underestimate downside risks. This results in portfolio underperformance compared to a respective benchmark.
4. **Hold poorly diversified portfolios:** Overconfident investors hold on to their favourite company's stocks, resulting in under-diversified portfolios. This may also result in unknowingly assuming more risk than normally permitted.

## Diagnostic Testing

These questions are designed to detect cognitive errors stemming from overconfidence bias. To complete the test, select the option that best characterises your response to each item.

**Question 1:** Global Financial Crisis (GFC) of 2008-09 seriously disrupted many economies and markets. How easy do you think it was to predict GFC?

a) Difficult.

b) Somewhat easy.

c) Easy.

**Question 2:** Relative to other drivers on the road, how good a driver are you?

a) Bad.

b) Average.

c) Above average.

**Test Result Analysis**

For both questions, people choosing option 'c' are susceptible to overconfidence bias.

**Mitigating Strategies for Overconfidence Bias**

1. **Performance evaluation:** Trading records should be reviewed at periodical intervals for identifying the winners and losers. Loss-making decisions should be examined to discover patterns and common mistakes. Similarly, the gains should be carefully analysed to ascertain if those gains resulted from the skills of the manager or luck.

2. **Investment policy and strategic asset allocation:** Formulate an investment policy statement (IPS) after carefully considering situational and psychological profiling on one hand and the long-term financial goals on the other. Strategic asset allocation (SAA) grounded on such investment policy plays a pivotal role in satisfying investor's long-term financial goals. Therefore, rather than focusing on short-term market noises, the investor should follow IPS and SAA in a disciplined manner to meet defined financial goals.

3. **Don't compare yourself to others:** One must remember that each one is unique in terms of talents, skills, and goals. The overconfidence can be avoided

if one assumes modesty with enthusiasm.

4. **Seek important feedback:** One should consciously seek feedback on one's investment models, strategies, and processes and listen to constructive criticism from advisors or people within the trusted circle.

5. **Stay away from irrational exuberance:** We often hear people trying to imitate big bulls such as Warren Buffet and Rakesh Jhunjhunwala, who have been successful with investing in the capital market. These are the people with unique talent and have worked hard to reach the current level of success. Rather than dreaming of becoming successful like these star investors, one should stick to one's financial planning and asset allocation in a disciplined manner.

Financial advisors have a key role to guard investors against overconfidence bias by educating them on how to stay on course with financial planning and strategic asset allocation to optimise investments.

## 18

# Self-Control Bias

*"The market, like the Lord, helps those who help themselves."*

—Robert G. Hagstrom

Self-control bias highlights the trade-off between current consumption and saving enough for future retirement. Simply put, self-control bias is a human behavioural tendency that causes people to consume today at the expense of saving for tomorrow. In the world of personal finance, self-control can take many forms, such as spending too high a percentage of income or, even worse, taking on too much debt.

Self-control bias is best understood in the context of the life-cycle hypothesis, which describes a well-defined link between the savings and consumption tendencies of individuals through different stages of life—childhood, years of work participation, and retirement. The income profile starts with low income during the early working years and is followed by increasing income that reaches a peak prior to retirement. Income during retirement, based on assumptions regarding pensions, is likely to be substantially lower. To make up for the lower income during retirement and be able to maintain a similar lifestyle, individuals will have to save a fraction of their income when they are still working in order to spend it later during retirement.

Studies have shown that people who do not plan for retirement are much less likely not to retire securely than those who plan for retirement. Planning is a vital key for attaining long-term financial goals. Further, financial plans need to be written down so that they can be reviewed on a regular basis. Without planning, investors may not be apt to invest in equities, potentially causing a problem as wealth will not be able to keep up with inflation. In summation, the following proverb holds true: "People do not plan to fail; they simply fail to plan."

## Example of Self-Control Bias

### Global Financial Crisis (2008-09)

One of the glaring examples of self-control bias is the global financial crisis (GFC) of 2008-09. GFC was triggered by massive borrowing gone wrong. During the first six years of the 21st century, the mortgage credit with low credit scores (sub-prime sector) in the USA grew more than twice as fast in neighbourhoods with high credit scores—a marked departure from the experience of previous decades. When the housing bubble burst, the economic consequences were sharply magnified by the way debt was distributed across households and communities. So much credit was available that people could not resist taking it on, and the result was one of the largest financial crises in history.

## Impact of Self-Control Bias on Investments

Given below is a summary of self-control bias behaviours that can trigger investment mistakes:

1. People need to have self-discipline imposed on them in order to save consistently. Self-control bias can cause investors to spend more today at the expense of saving for tomorrow. This behaviour can be disastrous and often leads people to adopt inappropriate degrees of risk in their portfolios in an effort to make up for the lack of savings which, in turn, can further aggravate the problem.
2. Self-control bias may cause investors to fail to plan for retirement. Studies have shown that people who do not plan for retirement are far less likely to retire securely as compared to those who have a retirement plan. Studies have also shown that people who do not plan for retirement are also less likely to invest in equity securities and thus becoming financially insecure due to the impact of inflation.
3. Self-control bias can cause asset-allocation imbalance problems. For example, some investors prefer income-producing assets, due to a 'spend today' mentality. This behaviour can be hazardous to long-term wealth creation. Too many income-producing assets can inhibit a portfolio to keep up with inflation.
4. Self-control bias can cause investors to lose sight of basic financial principles, such as compounding of

interest, dollar (or INR) cost averaging, and similar discipline behaviours that, if adhered to, can help create significant long-term wealth.

**Diagnostic Testing**

These questions are designed to detect cognitive errors stemming from self-control bias. To complete the test, select the option that best characterises your response to each item.

**Question 1:** Suppose that your 5-years old car is creating some troubles and you decide to buy a new car but face some constraints in your expenditure budget. You have an option to either go for a budget car or a costly luxury model. Which of the following approaches are you most likely to take?

a) I would typically not overspend on a car because I view a car as a means of transportation only.
b) I would typically purchase a medium-priced model with some fancy options, simply because I enjoy a nice car. I may forgo other purchases in order to afford a nice car.
c) When it comes to cars, I like to indulge myself. I would probably buy the most luxurious model, even at the expense of saving money for the long-term requirement.

**Question 2:** How would you characterise your retirement savings patterns?

a) I consult my advisors, ensure to take advantage of tax-favoured investments, and at times, save additional funds in taxable accounts.

b) I usually take advantage of most tax-favoured investments but in some cases, I miss out. I may or may not save something in taxable investment accounts.

c) I hardly ever save for retirement. I spend most of my disposable income on current consumption.

**Question 3:** How well would you rate your own self-discipline?

a) I always achieve a goal if it is important to me. For example, if I want to lose weight, I will diet and exercise regularly.

b) I often attain my goals, but sometimes, I am unable to accomplish my goals.

c) I find it difficult to keep my promises and follow a disciplined routine. I often find myself reaching out to others for help in order to attain key goals.

### Test Results Analysis

People answering 'b' or 'c' to any of the above questions may be susceptible to self-control bias.

### Mitigating Strategies for Self-Control Bias

A few common strategies noted below can help to counter the pitfalls of self-control bias.

1. **Planning:** After recognising self-control bias, it is important to put a financial plan in place. Your financial plan should be written down so that it can be reviewed at regular intervals. Just like in our day-to-day life, we mark the calendar to attend to our important appointments and make lists to help us remember what to buy at the grocery store, we also need to adhere to financial planning and invest in a disciplined manner for a comfortable retired life.
2. **Portfolio allocation:** Self-control bias can cause an imbalance in asset allocation. Temptations to 'spend today, think later' can result in income-producing assets and thus prevent a portfolio from growing and keeping up with inflation. Advisors must emphasise the importance of adhering to a strategic asset allocation, keeping with the client's long-run objectives. Irrespective of asset classes in the portfolio, clients exhibiting a lack of self-control need to be counselled about maintaining balanced portfolios so that they can attain their long-term financial goals.
3. **Control over spending:** Self-control bias can cause investors to spend more today instead of saving up for tomorrow. This behaviour can be counterproductive for maintaining long-term financial goals because retirement often arrives before investors have managed to save enough money. Advisors should counsel their clients for consistently setting aside a certain amount of money to ensure sufficient corpus for retirement. A careful balance must be struck

between saving, investing (in income and growth assets), and risk-taking in order to increase resources for retirement.

4. **Benefits of discipline:** Self-control bias can cause investors to lose sight of basic financial disciplines, such as compounding of interest or rupee cost averaging. Without discipline in investments, people can miss opportunities to accumulate significant long-term wealth. Therefore, it is essential for the advisor to counsel the clients on the benefits of compounding.

## 19

# Optimism Bias

*"When investing, pessimism is your friend,*
*euphoria the enemy."*
—Warren Buffett

Optimism bias (also known as the optimistic bias) is a cognitive bias that causes us to believe that our chances of experiencing positive events are higher while the chances of experiencing negative events are lower than those of our peers. Optimism bias is a common phenomenon and transcends gender, ethnicity, nationality, and age. It is sometimes also referred to as the *illusion of invulnerability* or *unrealistic optimism.*

While we often like to think of ourselves as highly rational and logical, researchers have found that the human brain is sometimes too optimistic for its own good. In fact, a growing body of scientific evidence points to the conclusion that optimism may be hardwired by evolution into the human brain. Due to this bias, when people are asked to estimate how likely they are to experience divorce, illness, job loss, or an accident, they are likely to underestimate the probability of such events ever impacting their lives. The fact is that we believe that we will live longer than average, that our children will be smarter than average, and that we will be more successful than average. But by definition, we cannot all be above average.

Looking from the perspective of behavioural finance, optimism bias has both virtues and pitfalls. On one hand, this bias protects and inspires people to keep moving forward in life and profession. It motivates people to assume risk and pursue goals. Optimists in general work longer hours, earn and save more. By believing that they are unlikely to fail and more likely to succeed, they have better self-esteem, lower stress levels, and better overall well-being.

But on the other hand, overly positive assumptions can lead to disastrous miscalculations which make people less likely to get health checkups, apply sunscreen, or open a savings account. In terms of the financial portfolio, it makes people more likely to bet on a bad investment. Undue optimism can also be financially harmful because it creates the illusion of having some unique insights or upper hand. Often, people at some level believe that they can see inaccurately priced securities, when in fact, they cannot. Therefore, it becomes of crucial importance to keep a check on this bias and adopt necessary mitigating strategies to keep it at bay.

**Examples of Optimism Bias**

Some examples of optimism bias are:

1. People believing that they have a lower risk of being a crime victim.
2. Smokers believing that they are less likely to contract lung cancer or disease as compared to other smokers.

3. First-time bungee jumpers believing that they have a lower risk of an injury as compared to other jumpers.
4. Traders who think they are less exposed to potential losses in the markets.

## Impact of Optimism Bias on Investments

Given below are some common investment mistakes caused by optimism bias:

1. **Employer's stock:** Optimism bias can cause investors to think that the company they work for is better than other companies in terms of overall prospects. They also grow greater comfort and optimism with the stock of their employer. As such, they normally tend to overweight the company stock in their portfolio.
2. **Portfolio return:** Optimism bias often leads investors to believe they are getting marketlike returns. However, the investors need to be more focused on the after-tax real returns on a long-term basis.
3. **Favourable prediction:** Optimism bias can sway investors to only view favourable forecasts such as positive earnings estimate of analysts or their own research. Additionally, investors prefer to get good news about the market and their investments and so maybe predisposed to optimism versus pessimism.
4. **Overestimating own skills:** Optimism bias can cause investors to think that they are above average investors. They tend to suffer from the illusion that

they are blessed with relatively better knowledge, skills, and competence in financial as well as social life.

5. **Home bias:** Optimism bias can cause investors to primarily invest near their geographic region because they may be unduly optimistic about the prospect of their local geographic area. By not investing outside their own region, they miss out on opportunities available elsewhere.

### Diagnostic Testing

These questions are designed to detect cognitive errors stemming from optimism bias. To complete the test, select the answer option that best characterises your response to each item.

**Question 1:** Relative to other drivers on the road, how good a driver are you?

a) Below average.

b) Average.

c) Above average.

**Question 2:** How optimistic are you about the investing opportunities close to home versus those overseas?

a) I am much more optimistic about investment opportunities close to home.

b) I am optimistic about investment opportunities in foreign locations.

c) I am neutral between investment opportunities close to home and in foreign locations.

**Question 3:** Relative to other investors, how good an investor are you?

a) Below average.
b) Average.
c) Above average.

**Test Results Analysis**

Question 1 and 3: People who select the option 'b' or 'c' are likelier to suffer from optimism bias.

Question 2: People who select the option 'a' indicate susceptibility to optimism bias.

## Mitigating Strategies for Optimism Bias

In order to optimise investment portfolios, the investors need to keep track of the following strategies:

1. **Disciplined approach towards savings:** Saving and investing are the keys to attain long-term financial goals. Excessive optimism can lead to risky and suboptimal portfolio choices that do not align with their one's goals. In order to overcome optimism bias, people should try to save regularly in a disciplined manner. Rather than focusing on short-term plans, they should focus on long-term investment opportunities based on independent research.

2. **Strategic asset allocation:** Optimism bias can cause investors to excessively favour certain asset classes, while neglecting others. Advisors should encourage clients to build balanced asset allocation aligned to individual risk and return objectives.
3. **Compounding impact on long-term success:** Optimism bias can obscure the benefits of disciplined investing. Thus, it is of vital importance to encourage clients to let their money accumulate and compound year after year, like the dieting and exercise analogies.
4. **Financial advisor:** In order to overcome the negative impact of optimism bias, investors should use the services of a professional financial advisor who can plan, monitor, review the investment portfolio, and thus help them to achieve their financial goals.

## 20

# Loss Aversion Bias

*"The concept of loss aversion is certainly the most significant contribution of psychology to behavioural economics."*

—Daniel Kahneman

Loss aversion, a powerful emotional bias, arises from feeling more pain from a loss than pleasure from an equal gain. As demonstrated by Amos Tversky and Daniel Kahneman in 1992, the key idea behind the loss aversion bias is that people react differently to positive and negative changes to their status quo. More specifically, losses are twice as powerful compared to equivalent gains. It is worth mentioning that when Richard Thaler won the Nobel Prize in economics in 2017, the phrase 'loss aversion' appeared 24 times in the Nobel Prize committee's description of his contributions to science.

Loss aversion bias can make investors dwell excessively on risk avoidance when evaluating possible gains, since avoiding a loss is a more urgent concern than seeking a profit. When their investments do begin to succeed, loss-averse individuals hasten to lock in profits, fearing that the market might reverse itself and rescind their returns. The problem here is that divesting prematurely to protect gains limits upside potential. In essence, loss aversion bias causes investors to hold on to their losing investments and sell their winning ones, leading to suboptimal portfolio returns.

**Examples of Loss Aversion Bias**

1. People prefer to invest in safer bank fixed deposits providing low after-tax returns. They avoid investing in blue-chip stocks that carry higher risk but provide more attractive long-term returns.
2. Not selling a stock that one holds when the current rational analysis of the stock clearly indicates that one should exit from the investment.
3. Selling a stock that has gone up slightly in price just to realise a gain of any amount, when the analysis indicates that the stock should be held longer for a much larger profit.

**Impact of Loss Aversion Bias on Investments**

The list below summarises some common investment mistakes linked to loss aversion bias.

1. **Holding on to losing investments:** The tendency among investors to hold on to losers for too long has been attributed to loss aversion bias. Selling a losing stock crystalises the loss and triggers negative emotions. To avoid this, investors hold on to losing investments in the hope that the losses will be recovered in future periods. This behaviour has seriously negative consequences and depresses portfolio returns.

2. **Selling winning investments early:** The investors tend to sell winners too quickly in the fear that their profit will evaporate in future. This behaviour limits the upside potential of a portfolio. Also, trading too much for small gains which raises transaction costs can lead to lower investment returns.
3. **Assume more risk:** Loss aversion bias can cause investors to unknowingly assume more risk in their portfolio as they continue to hold assets that have deteriorated in quality and lost value. If an initial decline in value occurs, then investors assume excessive risk in the hope of recovery and return to the psychologically set reference point.
4. **Unbalanced portfolios:** As mentioned above, loss aversion bias leads the investor to sell the winners and hold on to the losers in a falling market. This results in portfolio imbalance, and without proper rebalancing, the allocation becomes unsuitable for the long-term goals of the client, leading to suboptimal returns.

**Diagnostic Testing**

These questions are designed to detect signs of emotional bias stemming from loss aversion. To complete the test, select the option that best characterises your response to each item.

**Question 1:** Suppose you have invested in a stock that has gradually fallen 25% in value in the first six months. Most of the brokers have neutral or hold rating regarding it. You are unsure whether the stock will recover. What will you do?

a) I will hold on to the stock because it is better to wait till the stock recovers.

b) I will sell, book loss, and reinvest the proceeds in another stock.

**Question 2:** Suppose you have invested INR 100,000 and are presented with two alternatives given below. Which scenario would you rather have?

a) Get an assurance that I will be repaid INR 90,000 for sure.

b) Take a 50-50 gamble, knowing that I will get back either INR 120,000 or INR 80,000.

**Test Results Analysis**

Question 1: People who are loss averse are most likely to select the option 'a', even though option 'b' would be a more prudent strategy considering the risk of holding the loser.

Question 2: In this scenario, most people would probably select the option 'b' because they tend to be loss averse. Loss-averse investors are willing to gamble and risk an even greater loss rather than to admit a loss (option 'a').

**Mitigating Strategies for Loss Aversion Bias**

1. **Stop-loss limit:** Holding losing stocks for too long is harmful for your investment health. One effective remedy is setting up a stop-loss rule. You may, for

example, agree to sell a security immediately if it incurs a 10 per cent loss. However, it is best to consider an investment's expected levels of volatility when devising a stop-loss rule. You do not want to be forced to sell if an investment's price is just exhibiting its customary ups and downs. Volatility is a fact of life in equity.

2. **Book-profit limit:** Loss aversion can cause investors to sell winning positions too early, fearing that their profits will evaporate otherwise. This behaviour limits the upside potential of a portfolio and can lead to overtrading and lower returns. Just as stop-loss rules can help an exit from losing investments, it is helpful to set book-profit limits for selling appreciating investments. This will enable to let gains reach a meaningful profit level before the exit call is triggered. It is important to keep in mind the tax effect before profit booking.

3. **Portfolio management process:** The pain of loss can cause investors to hold on to losing investments. To mitigate this, a disciplined well thought out investment management process should be set in place. This should set out defined criteria for booking investment (example, expected return, standard deviation, credit rating, buy/sell/hold ratings, etc.) as well as exiting the investment (example, stop-loss and book-profit limits). Such a framework will enable the investor to make the right decision to protect the overall portfolio and avoid acting from a place of loss aversion.

4. **Diversified portfolios:** "Don't put all your eggs in one basket," goes the saying. Diversification is the practice of spreading one's investments around so that the exposure to any one type of asset is limited. However, loss aversion bias often causes investors to hold concentrated loss-making investments with strong emotions attached. This calls for investor education about the benefits of asset allocation and diversification. In this context, a useful question for the investor is: "If you didn't own any ABC stock today, would you still want to pick up as many shares as you own right now?" If the answer is no, then the portfolio should be rebalanced and the loss-making investments should be replaced by high-quality investments.

# 21

# Case Studies: Behaviourally Modified Asset Allocation

*"Bull markets are born in pessimism, grow on skepticism, mature on optimism and die on euphoria."*

—John Templeton

This chapter provides a basic framework for applying behavioural finance in a real-life setting. In earlier chapters, a foundation of behavioural finance has been laid with discussion on nineteen most dominant behavioural biases, covering a general description, examples, impact of the bias on investments, diagnostic test, and mitigating strategies to overcome the pitfalls of related biases. The current chapter aims to put all the concepts from traditional and behavioural finance space together and construct a few case studies to demonstrate how investors and practitioners can use such knowledge in portfolio management. The outline of the chapter is as follows:

1. Traditional Finance: Mean-Variance Optimisation
2. Investment: Portfolio Management
3. Integrating Traditional and Behavioural Finance

4. Behaviourally Modified Asset Allocation (BMAA)
5. Hypothetical Case Studies A-D
6. Summary

## 1. Traditional Finance: Mean-Variance Optimisation

Traditional finance assumes that individuals are risk-averse, have all the required information, and focus on maximising their personal utility function. The goal of mean-variance optimisation in modern portfolio theory is to maximise an investment's reward based on its risk. An optimised portfolio should generate the highest possible return based on an investor's chosen amount of risk. All things being equal, when two securities have the same expected return, you should select the one with the lower variance. Likewise, when two assets have the same variance, you should select the one with the higher expected return.

## 2. Investment: Portfolio Management

Investment (Portfolio Management) broadly follows a 3-step process:

**2.1 Planning:** Collecting client's personal and financial information, setting up individual goals, determination of risk tolerance and required return, investment policy formulation, strategic asset allocation, and allocation of funds among different asset classes are integral steps for holistic planning. Investors can choose from a range of asset classes, i.e., traditional assets like equity, bond (fixed income), cash (including bank deposits), and other alternative investments such as real estate, commodities, hedge funds, private equity, etc. Investors can also opt for value-based investing such as socially responsible investment (SRI), environmental, social, and governance (ESG) investment, green and sustainability investment, etc.

**2.2 Execution of portfolio decisions:** Portfolio implementation is the second important step. Knowledgeable and skilled investors can directly implement (buying and selling of assets/ securities) themselves. Others can invest through a professional portfolio manager like MF (Mutual fund), PMS (Portfolio management services), AIF (Alternative investment funds), etc. One of the key factors to consider here is the transaction costs and the expense ratio.

**2.3 Performance, review, and rebalancing:** Performance evaluation is the last step when it comes to portfolio management and involves measurement and appraisal of performance. A review should be done periodically to ensure portfolio performance is in line with the objectives and constraints set out in the investment policy. Any divergence between the target and actual portfolio performance may call for a rebalancing of the portfolio.

## 3. Integrating Traditional and Behavioural Finance

The mean-variance optimisation strategy of portfolio management does not consider the behavioural biases of the investor. Many advisors first administer a risk tolerance questionnaire, then discuss the client's financial goals and constraints, and finally recommend the asset allocation based on mean-variance optimisation. In the absence of any other diagnostic analysis, this methodology is certainly useful and generates important information. However, there are a few factors that restrict the usefulness of risk tolerance questionnaires. Several recent studies suggest that individual behavioural preferences (biases) should be accounted for in order to optimise asset allocation processes.

Looking from a portfolio perspective, a behaviourally adjusted asset allocation could move up or down from the mean-variance optimised portfolio to accommodate behavioural biases. Normally, such deviation should not stray more than 20 per cent from the mean-variance optimised allocation. For example, if a mean-variance optimised portfolio comprises 60 per cent equities and 40 per cent fixed-income instruments, a practitioner could make routine discretionary adjustments, resulting in a 50 to 70 per cent in equities and 30 to 50 per cent in bonds (fixed income). The rationale for the 20 per cent figure is that most investment policy statements permit discretionary asset class ranges of 10 per cent in either direction. Besides, the total behavioural factor (TBF), i.e., the sum of per cent change from the mean-variance output in respect of all assets would ideally be restricted to a 20 per cent corridor.

Given every investor is unique in terms of financial goals, risk tolerance, asset class preferences. etc., it is almost impossible to determine a one-size-fits-all solution towards portfolio construction. But the broad objective is to decide on an asset allocation that helps the client to attain financial goals while simultaneously providing enough psychological comfort.

## 4. Behaviourally Modified Asset Allocation (BMAA)

In the planning step, strategic asset allocation, i.e., allocation of funds among different asset classes, plays a vital role in converting the investor's objectives, constraints, and long-term capital market expectations into an appropriate portfolio. Behaviourally modified asset allocation (BMAA) is the best possible practical asset allocation which helps the client to attain their financial goals, while simultaneously providing enough psychological comfort. The key challenge before constructing a BMAA is when to moderate and when to adapt to the investor's biases.

Michael M. Pompian, one of the leading proponents of behavioural finance, in his book *Behavioural Finance and Wealth Management*, offers some insights through the following suggestions:

- **Principle I: Moderate Biases in Less Wealthy Clients, Adapt to Biases in Wealthier Clients**

  In the case of less wealthy clients, the major risk is longevity risk, i.e., the risk of the client outliving the assets. If a biased allocation could put a client's way of life at risk, moderating the bias is required. In the case of financially secure/wealthier clients, adapting to the client's biases is the appropriate course of action.

- **Principle II: Moderate Cognitive Biases, Adapt to Emotional Biases**

  Behavioural biases fall into two broad categories—cognitive and emotional. Cognitive biases stem from faulty reasoning and can be corrected with better information and advice. Emotional biases, on the other hand, originate from impulse or intuition rather than conscious reasoning and hence they are difficult to rectify. Cognitive biases include heuristics such as anchoring and adjustment, availability, confirmation, conservatism, framing, the illusion of control, mental accounting, representativeness, etc. Emotional biases include overconfidence, endowment, loss aversion, self-attribution, self-control, status quo, regret aversion, etc.

There will be cases where heeding principles I and II simultaneously would yield a blended combination. For example, a less-wealthy client with strong emotional biases should be both adapted and moderated. Additionally, there could be a scenario where two clients exhibiting similar biases should be advised differently.

## 5. Hypothetical Case Studies (A-D)

We will use four hypothetical case studies to simulate the approach for behaviourally adjusted asset allocation. All four cases will attempt to:

1. Identify the client's wealth level and behavioural biases.
2. Determine whether to moderate or adapt to client preference.
3. Formulate a quantitative guideline methodology and recommend the best practical asset allocation.

**Background**

For each of the four case studies, let us assume the year is 2015. A new national government in India with a record majority has assumed office in 2014. The high inflation and low growth witnessed in 2013 are now behind. There is an air of hope, aspiration, and expectation of higher growth and economic prosperity among people. For the sake of simplicity, let us assume the asset allocation will be divided between stocks, bonds, and cash.

- **Case A: Mr Ganapati Raju**

Mr Ganapati Raju (hereafter referred as 'Mr G') is a 67-year-old successful Indian entrepreneur. He is the founder and managing director of Star Enterprises, a publicly listed company. The enterprise is engaged in the packing business and currently running successfully. Last year, Mr G had a mild heart attack, but he has made full recovery. After successfully leading Star Enterprises for almost four decades, he has decided to handover the job of managing Star Enterprises to a professional CEO and retires himself from active business. Mr G currently lives with his wife. His son (age 37) and daughter (age 32) are married and settled in the USA. Mr G enjoys travelling around the world and the cost of living expenses, including travelling, is estimated at INR 50 lakhs per year at current prices. Mr G lives in his own house in Malabar Hills, a posh locality in Mumbai, and also owns a farmhouse in Darjeeling. Apart from it, his wealth comprises INR 6 crore invested in bank deposits and government securities, about INR 34 crore (current market value) investment in two stocks, i.e., INR 24 crore in Star Enterprises and another INR 10 crore in a newly set up private equity (PE) fund.

Mr G's primary goal is to maintain his current standard of living. Despite a substantial drop in the value of Star Enterprise stocks over the last two years, Mr G is not inclined to sell any of the shares. He is proud of these stocks as they form a part of his life's entrepreneurial success. Besides, he thinks that he can sell the stocks at an opportune time at a 25% higher price from current level which was witnessed in the year 2017. You have been introduced to Mr G by a common friend and requested to advise him regarding a suitable investment plan.

**Behavioural Analysis**

You are concerned that a severe downturn in the equity market may cut into Mr G's wealth. Mr G's mean-variance optimised portfolio recommendation is 65 per cent stocks, 30 per cent bonds, and 5 per cent cash. This is a less aggressive portfolio and Mr G can still meet his primary financial objectives. Mr G's responses to the comprehensive behavioural bias questionnaire show his susceptibility to:

- *Availability bias* (the tendency to believe that what is easily recalled is more likely to happen).
- *Illusion of control bias* (a superstition that one can control, or at least influence, outcomes beyond their control).
- *Mental accounting bias* (mentally dividing investments to separate nonfungible buckets or accounts).

- *Anchoring bias* (expecting to sell the stocks at 2017 prices).

However, Mr G thinks that he is an exceptionally good investor. During your interaction, Mr G stated his desire of drawing from bank deposits and PE fund for daily expenses and foreign travels respectively. Given your interaction and the behavioural biases demonstrated by Mr G, you are considering the following questions:

1. What effect do Mr G's biases have on the asset allocation decision?
2. Should you moderate or adapt to his biases?
3. What is the best practical asset allocation for Mr G?

## Impact of Biases on Investments

Mr G's biases lead to an allocation dominated by equities. His risk-taking behaviour developed through years of managing business provides such comfort. His intention to sell the stocks only after significant appreciation in price, i.e., say 25 per cent higher (as witnessed a couple of years ago), indicates anchoring bias and illusion of control bias. His insistence on using investment in private equity fund towards foreign travels (mental accounting bias) does not factor in the liquidity risk attached to such investment. The current investments with the combined exposure of 85 per cent towards equity and private equity are excessive. Mr G has a high need for the current income to meet living and travel-related expenses. Therefore, even though his biases favour equity over bonds, there is a need for a more balanced portfolio with an allocation to bonds.

## Moderate or Adapt?

Considering his overall level of wealth, Mr G does not run a serious standard-of-living risk. His behavioural biases (anchoring bias, illusion of control bias, and mental accounting bias) are principally cognitive biases, suggesting that these can be moderated with additional information. While a complete adaptation would leave Mr G's current 85 per cent equity allocation, a complete moderation would imply the mean-variance optimised breakdown to be 65 per cent stocks, 30 per cent bonds, and 5 per cent cash. Taking into consideration Mr G's wealth level and bias profile, you prefer to moderate as well as adapt (some middle ground) as a best practical allocation.

## Best Practical Allocation Decision

The mean-variance optimised allocation you initially calculated for Mr G allocates is as follows: 65 per cent stocks, 30 per cent bonds, and 5 per cent cash. Mr G's higher risk tolerance and behavioural biases suit a portfolio with higher equity allocation. Considering Mr G's wealth level and the behavioural output received, you propose to modify allocation to 70 per cent stocks, 20 per cent bonds, and 10 per cent cash. Next, you run your behaviourally modified portfolio through Mr G and obtain his confirmation towards the changed asset allocation and the deviation from his current equity exposure of 85 per cent.

**Behaviourally Modified Asset Allocation (BMAA) for Mr Ganapati Raju**

| Asset Class | Allocation: Traditional Finance (%) (A) | Behavioural Factor (%) (B) | BMAA (A) + (B) |
|---|---|---|---|
| Equities | 65 | +5 | 70 |
| Bonds | 30 | -10 | 20 |
| Cash/Bank Deposit | 5 | +5 | 10 |
| | 100 | | 100 |
| Total Behavioural Factor (TBF): 5 + 10 + 5 = 20 | | | |

- **Case B: Mr K. Ramachandran**

Mr K Ramachandran (hereafter referred as 'Mr K') is a single 35-year-old IT executive working with a global information technology firm. He earns INR 50 lakhs per year. Mr K lives extravagantly and occasionally overspends, but he has saved approximately INR 1 crore. The primary financial goals of Mr K are to retire comfortably at 65 and donate INR 2 crores to his alma mater.

You have been working with Mr K for the last one year. You have drafted a financial plan but have yet to modify Mr K's pre-existing allocation (nearly 100 per cent equities).

However, you have developed a good working relationship with Mr K, and he listens intently and seems open to your recommendations. You also believe that Mr K has some behavioural issues to be addressed.

**Behavioural Analysis**

You propose a more conservative mean-variance optimised allocation (see table on page 175). However, you are worried that Mr K may not fully buy into the idea. Your concern is that a severe downward market fluctuation may cut into his wealth and daily living expenses, including possible health expenses. Your financial planning software tells you that with a less aggressive portfolio, Mr K can still meet his primary financial goals. However, Mr K thinks that he is a particularly good investor, and you are worried that such a change might cause him to regret not being more aggressive. He agrees to complete a comprehensive behavioural bias questionnaire and his results show susceptibility to:

- *Overconfidence bias* (the tendency to overestimate one's investment judgements).
- *Regret aversion bias* (the tendency to avoid deciding for fear that the decision may cause regret later).
- *Self-control bias* (the tendency to spend today rather than save for tomorrow).

**Behaviourally Modified Asset Allocation (BMAA) for Mr K. Ramachandran**

| Asset Class | Allocation: Traditional Finance (%) (A) | Behavioural Factor (%) (B) | BMAA (A) + (B) |
|---|---|---|---|
| Equities | 70 | +5 | 75 |
| Bonds | 25 | -10 | 15 |
| Cash/Bank Deposit | 5 | +5 | 10 |
| | 100 | | 100 |
| Total Behavioural Factor (TBF): 5 + 10 + 5 = 20 | | | |

The mean-variance optimised allocation you initially calculated for Mr K was 70 per cent stocks, 25 per cent bonds, and 5 per cent cash as Mr K's risk tolerance better suits a more balanced portfolio. You also have obtained confirmation of the specific behavioural biases that are probably causing the distortion in Mr K's portfolio. Your job is now to answer these questions:

1. What effect do Mr K's biases have on the asset allocation decision?
2. Should you moderate or adapt to his biases?
3. What is the best practical allocation for Mr K?

## Impact of Biases on Investment

Mr K's overconfidence bias raises his comfort level with stocks, perhaps excessively. He is also likely to regret missing out on any opportunities when equities surge and that he cannot fully exploit. But Mr K has also a high need for current income to fuel his 'spend today' mentality (self-control bias). Therefore, even though his biases favour equity over fixed income, they also imply a need for fixed-income investments. In the event of a market downturn, Mr K might have to rely on bonds to supplement his lifestyle.

## Moderate or Adapt?

Considering his overall level of wealth, Mr K does not run a serious standard-of-living risk with his present allocation, even in the event of a major market downturn. His behavioural biases are also principally emotional (regret aversion and self-control) which means one has to adapt to the recommendations.

It is important to note that adapting does not mean setting aside all behavioural considerations. You will need to create a portfolio more aggressive than the mean-variance optimiser suggests which will help Mr K to adhere comfortably to his allocation. However, at the same time, you will also need to run a cash flow analysis to ensure that your plan will not leave Mr K's living expenses at risk in case of a severe market downturn. You will also need to advise him to keep a comfortable cash reserve.

## Best Practical Allocation Decision

Referring to the case of Mr K. Ramachandran, the mean-variance-optimised allocation was 70 per cent stocks, 25 per cent bonds, and 5 per cent cash. However, using the guidelines presented earlier in the chapter, you devise the best practical allocation of 75 per cent stocks, 15 per cent bonds, and 10 per cent cash. Your financial planning software verifies that the new allocation should offer adequate living funds for Mr K, even if the market falls. In accordance with the total behavioural factor, you also confirm that your adjustment hasn't exceeded 20 per cent. You, therefore, present your recommendation to Mr K, explaining the rationale behind asset allocation strategy which deviates from his preference for 100 per cent equities.

- **Case C: The Mallik Family**

The Mallik family (hereafter referred as 'family') includes an educated couple (both aged 34) and their two children (aged 3 and 7). The family is financially sound but suffered badly during the global financial crisis in 2008-09. The couple's total annual income is INR 70 lakhs, which, like the family itself, is not expected to grow significantly. The family have managed to save INR 5.2 crore which they hope might serve as a financial foundation from which to send their children to college and, later, fund a comfortable retirement. You have been working with the family for three years. You update a financial plan for them annually and recommend an asset allocation. Previously, you suggested the allocation that the mean-variance optimiser generated: 70 per cent in equities, 25 per cent bonds, and 5 per cent cash. At that time, the family, however, chose to be more aggressive. This year, when you recommended the same mean-variance optimised allocation, the couple desired a more conservative position, requesting 50 per cent equities, 45 per cent bonds, and 5 per cent cash.

**Behavioural Analysis**

You have noticed that the family are trend followers. They are susceptible to short-lived market temptations. The family also tends to move in and out of asset classes in an effort to control their financial destiny. Predictably, they have not been too successful with their investments. This couple is typically not receptive to your advice. Currently, they have the idea that they should be in risk-averse investments (bonds), which have come into fashion following the last global financial meltdown. You decide to administer a behavioural bias test (for simplicity's sake, imagine that the couple completes the test jointly and share the same behavioural profile). You find that the family suffers from:

- *Illusion of control bias* (the superstition that they can control, or at least influence, outcomes beyond their control).
- *Recency bias* (mentally emphasising more recent events unduly with respect to less recent events).
- *Availability bias* (the tendency to believe that what is easily recalled is more likely to happen).

The family's mean-variance optimised portfolio recommendation is 70 per cent stocks, 25 per cent bonds, and 5 per cent cash. Given the biases they exhibit, you have the following questions before you:

- What effect do the family's biases have on the asset allocation decision?
- Should you moderate or adapt to their biases?
- What is the best practical allocation for the family?

**Impact of Biases on Investment**

The observed combination of biases suggests a clear allocation preference. Availability bias and recency bias leave the family preoccupied with the memories of the last global financial crisis. The memory of the financial meltdown prejudices them towards more conservative investments. Bonds also suit the family's illusions of control. The couple perceives that they will fare better with more direct command of their portfolio and that fixed-income securities are better suited as they are more predictable than equities. The diagnostic test results also throw insights as to why the family have swung towards such a conservative allocation.

**Moderate or Adapt?**

Illusion of control bias, recency bias, and availability bias are all cognitive biases, suggesting that they can be moderated with education and correct information. Furthermore, your financial planning software suggests that an insufficient equity allocation, given the family's modest level of wealth, might fail to cover college and retirement. You decide to moderate the family's biases, with the objective of increasing their equities allocation.

### Best Practical Allocation Decision

The mean-variance optimiser's recommended allocation was 70 per cent stocks, 25 per cent bonds, and 5 per cent cash. The family had previously contemplated dropping their equities allocation to 50 per cent after being influenced by the cognitive biases when they made this request. You also calculated that their conservative specified allocation would present a standard-of-living risk. Because the family's biases can perhaps be curbed by an educative discussion, and because you don't want to jeopardise their long-term financial goals, you stand firm and recommend the mean-variance optimised output as 70 per cent stocks, 25 per cent bonds, and 5 per cent cash. And because you haven't adapted this allocation by way of any adjustments, the total behavioural factor (TBF) in asset allocation is not required.

- **Case D: Mrs Lakshmi Bose**

Mrs Lakshmi Bose (hereafter referred as 'Mrs L') is a single, 68-year-old retiree, living a humble lifestyle. Her expenses are met from the only income generated from her investment portfolio valued at INR 1 crore at the current price. Your advisory relationship reveals that Mrs L's primary investment goal is for her investments to support her sustenance expenses for the rest of her life. She is afraid of losing money and clearly remembers how her relatives lost money in the stock market crash of 2008-09. You have noticed that Mrs L is also stubborn and a bit inflexible in her thinking, especially on the topics of finance and markets.

**Behavioural Analysis**

Mrs L's portfolio comprises only bank deposits and government bonds. You are concerned that inflation will eat away her limited resources and eventually cause her to outlive her assets. However, from your earlier interactions, you suspect her discomfort at the prospect of rebalancing her portfolio. In order to understand her behavioural biases, you ask Mrs L to take a 30-minute diagnostic test. Mrs L, after some repeated requests, agrees to a short test. The test results confirm that Mrs L demonstrates:

- *Loss aversion bias* (the tendency to feel the pain of losses more acutely than the pleasure of gains).
- *Anchoring and adjustment bias* (the tendency to automatically rely on present market levels as neutral benchmarks for predicting future market trends).
- *Status quo bias* (the desire to keep things as they are).

As part of your allocation review, you also administer a risk tolerance questionnaire to Mrs L. Her score helps you generate a mean-variance optimised portfolio recommendation as 70 per cent bonds, 20 per cent stocks, and 10 per cent cash. So, now that you know Mrs L can theoretically tolerate a riskier portfolio than her existing one, you become more convinced about the impact of her behavioural biases on her investments. Your job is now to address the following questions:

1. What effect do Mrs L's biases have on the asset allocation decision?
2. Should you moderate or adapt to her biases?
3. What is the best practical allocation for Mrs L?

**Impact of Biases on Investment**

Since the results of the diagnostic test reveal that Mrs L does not tolerate risk (loss aversion bias) and does not like change (status quo bias), she would naturally prefer the safe and secure asset allocation (100 per cent bank deposits and government bonds) that she now owns. Also, since the market has been highly volatile in recent months, Mrs L will likely make faulty conclusions regarding current and expected downward trending prices (anchoring and adjustment bias). She is likely to avoid exposure to equities and would be happy to retain current asset allocation. However, you need to bear in mind Mrs L's bias towards such an allocation and the longevity risk, i.e., the potential risk attached to the increasing life expectancy and the investor outliving the assets.

**Moderate or Adapt?**

You are concerned that Mrs L might outlive her assets if she adheres to her present allocation. Your financial planning software confirms your fears. Mrs L's level of wealth, while adequate at present, is not substantial enough to support her entire life. So, if you adapt to her biases and agree to continue with 100 per cent deposits and bonds then Mrs L's critical financial goal becomes jeopardised. However, Mrs L's biases are principally emotional (status quo and loss aversion bias) and typically cannot be corrected with advice and information. This will complicate things if you attempt to moderate her biases, given that Mrs L's wealth level is not excessive and her biases are primarily emotional.

Mrs L's case clearly yields a blended recommendation that you should moderate as well as adapt to her biases. This course of action, which might appear contradictory, is really more about compromise. A complete moderation of Mrs L's biases would imply a mean-variance optimised breakdown as 70 per cent bonds, 20 per cent equities, and 10 per cent cash. While a complete adaptation would preserve the allocation of 100 per cent bonds, moderating and adapting would require negotiating for some middle ground. Taking into consideration Mrs L's wealth level and bias profile, you now begin to draft the best practical allocation.

## Behaviourally Modified Asset Allocation (BMAA) for Mrs Lakshmi Bose

You decide that an allocation of 75 per cent bonds, 15 per cent stocks, and 10 per cent cash would approximate the mean-variance optimiser while also offering some concessions to Mrs L's conservatism. Then you check your financial planning software to discover that if she adopts this allocation, she will not outlive her money. Next, you run your behaviourally modified portfolio through the total behavioural factor and verify that the adjustment factor doesn't exceed the 20 per cent mark, a rule of thumb suggested by some experts. Since you have only corrected Mrs L's portfolio by 10 per cent, you are happy with that result. You present your recommendation to Mrs L and administer a continuing program of investor education on the risk of outliving one's assets going by her preference of 100 per cent in bonds.

| Asset Class | Allocation: Traditional Finance (%) (A) | Behavioural Factor (%) (B) | BMAA (A) + (B) |
|---|---|---|---|
| Equities | 20 | -5 | 15 |
| Bonds | 70 | +5 | 75 |
| Cash/Bank Deposit | 10 | 0 | 10 |
| | 100 | | 100 |
| **Total Behavioural Factor (TBF): 5 + 5 + 0 = 10** | | | |

**Summary**

**Life Cycle and Investment Cycle**

Ian E. Wilson, former chairman of GE, once said, "No amount of sophistication is going to allay the fact that all of your knowledge is about the past and all your decisions are about the future." The fact remains that the future is unknown. The way we view the future (uncertainties) reflects our biases. Trying to predict the future makes us anxious, especially when the future relates to money. One should deal with the future with the best possible realistic view of the probability, factoring the same into strategic asset allocation. Making money decisions requires clarity and once the goals are clearly defined and behavioural biases known, behaviourally modified asset allocation (BMAA) can be constructed as illustrated in the aforementioned case studies.

Concept adopted from book *Behavioural Finance and Wealth Management* by Michael M. Pompian

All the four case studies discussed in the chapter have been captured in the figure above. As an advisor, one may encounter cases resembling any or all the scenarios displayed. Even a mix of various cognitive and emotional biases is possible. Whatever scenario one encounters, it is hoped that the template methodology illustrated in the chapter can be tailored to any particular situation. In general, bias type and the wealth levels detect the desired strategy, i.e., whether to moderate or to adapt to a client. Sometimes, the mean-variance output will be enough. However, at other times, the behavioural modified asset allocation (BMAA) would need to be constructed by incorporating important behavioural biases and preferences.

While only traditional assets such as equity, bond, and cash have been considered in our examples, the asset classes could also be extended to include any other asset of client's preference, i.e., alternative investments such as precious metals, real estate, commodities, hedge funds, etc. or even value-based investing like socially responsible investment (SRI), environmental, social, and governance (ESG) investment, etc. In such a scenario, the asset class weights would be proportionately adjusted.

It may be noted that the BMAA, a convergence of traditional and behavioural finance, does not aim at a perfect portfolio or the highest return from the portfolio. Rather, it seeks to broadly align the investment cycle with the life cycle. In the long run, BMAA aims at ensuring financial security, liquidity, and sustainable returns and enabling the investor to move forward in life confidently.

## 22

# Behavioural Biases and Investment Processes

*"Most people spent most of their time and effort earning money and hardly any time managing and growing it."*

—Anonymous

The current chapter focuses on understanding how behavioural finance affects the market and various market practitioners. The chapter is organised as follows:

1. Market Behaviour
2. Financial Advisors
3. Analysts
4. Committees

### 1. Market Behaviour

Financial bubbles or subsequent crashes are periods of unusual positive or negative returns. These are triggered by panic buying (greed) or selling (fear), neither of which is supported by economic fundamentals. A bubble or crash is sometimes defined as an extended period of prices that are two standard deviations from the mean. A crash can also be characterised as a fall in asset prices of 30% or more over a period of several months.

(Adapted from Robert Rich, Hedgeye Risk Management, LLC)

Typically, an asset bubble occurs when the price of a financial asset or commodity rises to levels that are well above either historical levels or the asset's intrinsic value, or both. The problem is that since the intrinsic value of an asset can have a very wide range, a bubble is often justified by the flawed assumption that an asset's intrinsic value has skyrocketed, meaning the asset is worth much more than its fundamentally value. Recent bubbles were seen in the prices of technology during 1999-2000. The NASDAQ

Composite Index, home to most of these technology/dot-com company stocks, soared from a level of under 500 at the beginning of 1990 to a peak of over 5,000 in March 2000. Similarly the residential housing prices increased significantly in United States, United Kingdom, and Australia, culminating in the financial crises of 2008-2009. The average US home lost one-third of its value.

In India, the NIFTY index rose from around 1,100 as of March 31, 2002, to a high of 6,000 at the end of December 2007, thus posting a handsome CAGR return of 40 per cent during this period. The stock market exuberance was supported by easy liquidity, a surge in foreign capital inflows, and a high annual growth rate in the economy, averaging close to 9 per cent. In calendar year 2007, the NIFTY index posted a return of 54.8 per cent. Many first-time retail investors got enchanted by the compelling bull run and jumped into the stock market during the peak of 2007. Global stock markets dropped during the financial crisis in 2008-2009. NIFTY index crashed 51.8 per cent in 2008. The investors who entered the stock market in 2007, at the fag-end of the bull run and exited next year in panic, lost about half of their wealth.

There are several behavioural biases contributing to bubbles including:

- *Overconfidence bias* (underestimating risk and excessive trading, and believing 'it's different this time).
- *Confirmation bias* (investors accepts the evidence that justifies overvaluation and ignores evidence that contradicts their beliefs).

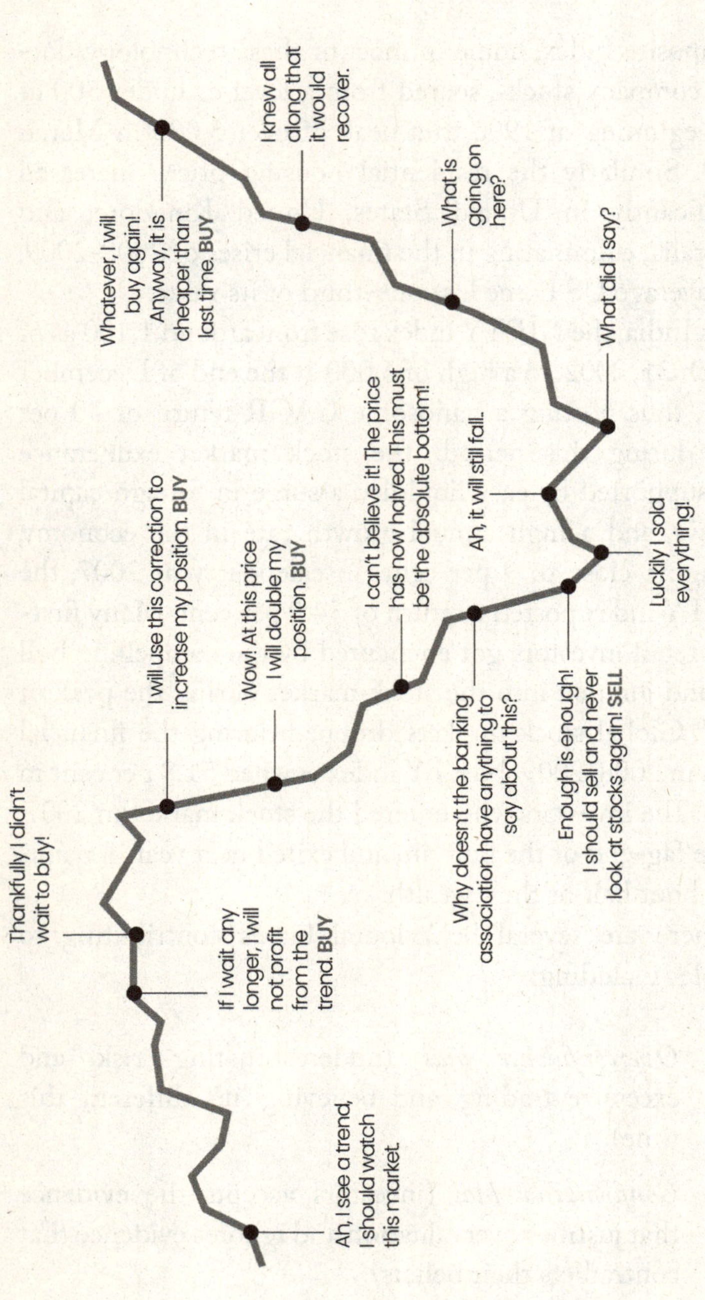


Concept adapted from: Credit Suisse; Behaviourial Finance: The Psychology of Investing

- *Self-attribution bias* (investors take personal credit for the success of their trades).
- *Regret aversion bias* (investors do not want to regret missing out on all the gains everyone else seems to be making).
- *Herding* (investors trade in the same direction or in the same securities and at times, contrary to the information available to them).
- *Recency bias* (recent information is given more importance because it is vividly remembered).

When it comes to the stock market, it always rallies strongly before a crash. Traditional valuation metrics can be used to identify extreme overvaluation. For example, an equity index trading at a price-to-earnings ratio that is twice the historical average is likely to be in bubble territory.

However, more analysis may be needed to make a conclusive determination. It is difficult to precisely forecast the point of reversal from bubble to crash, as this depends on a host of factors underlying human behaviour.

## 2. Financial Advisors

Behavioural finance is about understanding how people make decisions, both individually and collectively. As behavioural finance gains credibility and acceptance by the investment community, the advisors and investors are increasingly including behavioural considerations in the advisor-client relationship. This results in an investment portfolio that the client is comfortable with and will be happy staying in over the long term. The success of the advisor-client relationship can be measured in the following four distinct areas:

i. **Incorporating behavioural questions in risk tolerance questionnaires:** As one of the first steps in the client-advisor relationship protocol, a risk-tolerance questionnaire is normally filled out by the client. Such a questionnaire only indicates some behavioural traits but does not capture them. This needs to be amended by incorporating relevant diagnostic questions on the behavioural assessment. The responses from the questionnaire should provide holistic information including insights into the client's psychology (example, active or passive investor, overconfidence, loss aversion, etc.) which will help with a better understanding of the client's goals.
ii. **Formulating investment policy statement (IPS):** An investment policy statement (IPS) is a written planning document that governs all investment decisions of the client. This document integrates the client's needs, preferences, and circumstances into a statement of the client's objectives and constraints. The constraints section of IPS should clearly highlight any specific behavioural preference that the client has. Such additional information equips the advisor with insights into the factors behind the client's goals.
iii. **Professional relationship:** With a better understanding of behavioural finance vis-à-vis risk-taking, advisors can enhance their understanding

of client preferences and develop better-informed recommendations of investment strategies and products. Addressing client's expectations in a consistent manner is essential to a successful relationship. Thus, behavioural finance adds professionalism and structure to such a relationship, allowing advisors to better understand the client before delivering any investment advice.

iv. **Walking the client throughout the investment journey:** The investment is not a one-time event, but a journey. The primary benefit of incorporating behavioural finance into the client-advisor relationship is a closer bond between the two. By developing a comprehensive grasp of the client's motives and fears, the advisor can structure an appropriate behaviourally modified portfolio for the client with a periodical review to reflect the changes in the client's situation, market conditions, and the portfolio itself. Besides, the advisor can guide the client throughout the life's journey across market cycles. This results in happier clients and enhanced practice and career for the advisor.

### 3. Analysts

The experts in varying fields make forecasting errors as a result of behavioural biases. Financial analysts are also subject to the same bias. In fact, it is their superior skills in analysing companies that makes them also vulnerable to forecasting errors. An understanding of their weaknesses can help analysts limit the degree of their forecasting errors.

The three primary areas of behavioural biases that can affect analysts' forecasts are:

i. Overconfidence in forecasting skills

ii. Influence by company management

iii. Biased research

- **Overconfidence in Forecasting Skills**

Overconfidence is a key behavioural bias relevant to investment analysts. Overconfidence bias is a bias in which people demonstrate unwarranted faith in their own intuitive reasoning, judgements, and/or cognitive abilities. It may be the result of overestimating knowledge levels, abilities, and access to information. For example, people generally do a poor job of estimating probabilities but believe they do it well because they believe that they are smarter and more informed than they actually are. Overconfidence may be intensified when combined with self-attribution bias, where people take credit for successes and assign responsibility for failures to some external factors. There are several other behavioural biases that contribute to overconfidence, such as:

- Representativeness bias arises out of any additional information or detail which appears to conform to the overall scenario being forecast, even if it is largely irrelevant, and so adding to confidence in the forecast.
- Availability bias leads individuals to give undue weight to more accessible and readily recalled information.

- Illusion of control bias leads analysts to forecast complex patterns of business performance or stock price behaviour. They feel confident about their predictions on short- and long-term recommendations, price targets, and earnings forecasts.
- Hindsight bias can involve both cognitive and emotional bias. It is a result of the process of integrating new information with prior beliefs. A source of error in calibrating earlier forecasts typically arises from selective recall, in which individuals remember showing greater foresight than proved to be the case.

## Remedial Actions

Dealing with overconfidence bias is difficult. However, there are several actions analysts can take to minimise the errors in forecasts.

i. Good motivation can be achieved if an individual is directly accountable for accuracy to supervisors or clients. Getting prompt and immediate feedback through self-evaluations, colleagues, and superiors combined with a structure that rewards accuracy should lead to better self-calibration.

ii. Well-structured feedback can also reduce hindsight bias. An analyst should document a decision or forecast and the reasons for that judgement. A written record helps make the later evaluation more objective. Documenting the reasons for the judgement not only allows the accuracy to be assessed later but also why the decision was right or wrong.

iii. One method that can help reduce overconfidence is for an analyst to be required to provide at least one counterargument in the report. If the documentation of the research includes one good reason why the conclusion might turn out to be wrong, the forecasting accuracy can be improved and confidence can be better calibrated. When listing evidence for and against a conclusion, it is the evidence against that does the most good in countering overconfidence.

iv. Bayes' formula is a mathematical rule that explains how existing probability beliefs should be changed given new information. In other words, Bayes' formula expects people to update old beliefs in a certain manner when given new information. Bayes' formula can be a useful tool for analysis as it reduces the risk of behavioural biases in incorporating new information.

v. Analysts should also consider sample size. Basing forecasts on small samples can lead to unfounded confidence in unreliable models.

- **Influence by Company Management**

The way a company's management presents/frames the information can influence how analysts interpret it and include it in their forecasts. In such a case, analysts should remember three prominent cognitive biases—*anchoring and adjustment bias, availability bias,* and *framing bias.*

1. Framing refers to a person's tendency to interpret the same information differently based on how it is presented.
2. Anchoring means that the framework for interpreting and analysing the available information can be influenced disproportionately by an initial, default position or anchor. This anchor can be chosen in a variety of ways. For example, a management presentation describing specific successes or selecting favourable comparisons for business performance could anchor an analyst's view of the business results as successful.
3. Subsequently, less favourable metrics or explanations might not be given the appropriate consideration or weight, leading to a skewed picture of the situation. Analysts should recognise the risk of such incomplete information being given undue importance in the analysis relative to the analyst's own ratios and metrics.

**Remedial Actions**

i. Focusing on metrics and comparable data, rather than what is descriptive or unverifiable can assist forecast accuracy and consistency of approach across research.

ii. Calibration of likely accuracy can be improved by framing the issue appropriately, gathering information, and recognising underlying base rates.

- **Biased Research**

Collecting too much unstructured information, the illusion of control, overconfidence, representativeness, confirmation bias, and gambler fallacy are some of the usual biases related to analysts performing research.

- Confirmation bias, a cognitive bias, is the tendency for people to misread evidence as additional support for an initial hypothesis. The additional information may not be analysed in a rigorous way, but it can nevertheless appear to make the judgement or forecast more likely by sharing some of its general characteristics.
- The gamblers' fallacy, a related to cognitive bias (Shiffrin 2007), refers to a misunderstanding of probabilities in which people wrongly project reversal to a long-term mean. Investment professionals and strategists in particular can suffer from this cognitive bias. It reflects a faulty understanding of the behaviour of random events, expecting reversals to occur more frequently than actually happens. With the gamblers' fallacy, the analyst expects a pattern that has diverged from the long-term average to reverse within a specific period of time. Another fallacy, common to gamblers and many others, is the hot hand fallacy. People affected by this fallacy wrongly project the continuation of a recent trend. Both of these fallacies demonstrate a lack of understanding of statistical independence.

- Similar to endowment bias, assets may be endowed with additional value based on an emotional response. Analysts can associate financially sound companies with good or safe characteristics, although the external economic environment or high stock price for the company can make it risky. This view can also reflect *a confirmation bias.* Analysts may look for and notice what confirms their beliefs and ignore or undervalue what contradicts their beliefs.
- Studies have suggested that analysts have biases favouring growth over value. Earnings growth records themselves can be seen as representative of a growth business and naively extrapolated. The tendency of analysts to recommend high-growth and low-yield stocks typically reflects a failure to incorporate the base rate or effect of the environment in which a company operates. This situation may reflect a *representativeness bias.*

**Remedial Actions**

i. Given the errors and overconfidence in forecasts, analysts should focus on more objective data such as trailing earnings. However, even reported earnings may be affected by operating and accounting choices made by management. In making forecasts, analysts should evaluate previous forecasts and be wary of *anchoring and adjustment bias.*

ii. Emotional biases are difficult to deal with and can impact the research process and compromise any subsequent analysis. The solution is to collect information in a systematic way, and whenever possible, use metrics and ratios that allow comparability with historical trends and industry average.

iii. A search process should involve seeking contrary facts and opinions. Analysts should get prompt feedback that allows them to re-evaluate their opinions and gain knowledge for future reference, all the while documenting the entire process.

**4. Committees**

Many investment decisions are taken by groups or committees rather than by individuals acting alone (example, research committee approving stock recommendations, investment club deciding which stock to buy, board of trustees deciding on pension plan decisions, etc.). The idea behind such committee decisions is that the collective expertise of individual members will contribute to better investment decision-making. However, as studies indicate, the individual biases mentioned before can be either diminished or amplified along with additional biases being created.

At times, the decision-making process in a group setting is poor due to a number of behavioural factors, such as individuals are biased to follow the opinion of a group *(social proof bias)*, group dynamics inhibit individuals to share relevant information, and individuals tend to support a dominant member's views or opinions.

## Remedial Actions

i. Committee chair should encourage other members to speak out even if the member's views are contrary to the group's views.

ii. Members should be selected from diverse backgrounds and cultures.

iii. Committees can collect members' views before a discussion begins.

iv. Committees should promote mutual respect for all the members of the group.

23

# The Journey into Future

*"Wealth is the ability to fully experience life."*
—Henry David Thoreau

Congratulations! You have now reached the last chapter of the book. Whether you have already read previous chapters or randomly flipped to this page, you have arrived just in time for a meeting of minds as we set out on our journey of self-discovery. While we discussed extensively the behavioural aspects affecting the investment decisions of an investor in earlier chapters, you might also be interested to know about some basics of investment like setting an investment goal and building a portfolio to attain that objective. This concluding chapter attempts to integrate behavioural finance with the fundamentals of the life cycle and investment cycle from the perspective of a common investor. The chapter covers the following:

1. Life Cycle and Financial Planning
2. Investment Cycle and Asset Allocation Strategies
3. Future of Behavioural Finance
4. Concluding Remarks

## Life Cycle and Financial Planning

### 1.1 Life Cycle

Life consists of journeying into the future, and just like a traveller, each one of us has to carry with us some basic necessities to make our journey enjoyable. The majority of people think of the word 'wealth' in terms of finances only, but this is a narrow view. The timeless wisdom from our scriptures has conceptualised different types of wealth, especially comprising the following accomplishments:

- Physical wealth (health, nutrition, sleep, exercises, healthy habits, etc.)
- Financial wealth (income, expenditure, planning, investing, wealth creation, etc.)
- Emotional wealth (family, friends, people, positive thinking, wisdom, etc.)
- Social wealth (esteem, character, relationships, social service, charity, etc.)

While the book primarily focuses on financial wealth and portfolio management, one needs a harmonious blend of all the above mentioned types of wealth to lead a complete and fulfilling life. It is important to note that one cannot always buy physical, social, or emotional wealth with money. Rather, it requires careful attention, periodic introspection, and corrective actions to ensure that all types of wealth are earned and maintained for a life blessed with health, wealth, happiness, peace, and prosperity.

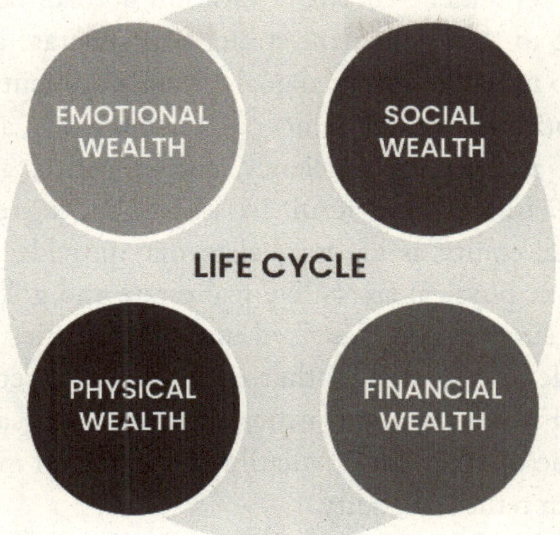


## 1.2 Financial Planning

Financial planning is the process of developing a personal roadmap for your financial well-being. The inputs to the financial planning process are one's finances, i.e., income, assets and liabilities, goals, current responsibilities, future financial needs, and appetite for risk. The output of the financial planning process is a personal financial plan (also known as *investment policy*) that guides how to use one's money to achieve short-term and long-term goals, while keeping in mind inflation, real returns, taxes, time horizon, and unique circumstances.

### *1.2.1 Financial Goals*

The financial goals aim at relieving a family of its financial responsibilities and achieving their dreams and aspirations. These goals can include children's higher education, buying a house, retirement corpus, a vacation abroad, etc. It has a linkage to the investment strategy to generate adequate wealth to meet the financial goals. The investment strategy must optimise on different parameters such as safety, liquidity, return, tax efficiency, risk appetite, and goal horizons. In the long term, in a fast-growing economy like India, equity as an asset class may provide a higher return over physical assets like real estate and gold as well as financial assets such as fixed income securities. But the other side of the coin is that equity as an asset class is volatile. Fixed income securities are considered safer than equity due to much lower volatility but may not match the long-term return of equity.

Once the financial goals have been decided, the next is the time horizon and the amount required to achieve the goals. Equity is advisable for longer-horizon goals. For shorter-horizon goals, fixed-income assets are a better option. The future amounts can be estimated with the current cost of goals and the inflation rate applicable to the category of expenses.

### *1.2.2 Life Stage Goals*

Life-changing events, such as getting married or joining a new job, will have financial implications on personal finance and investments. It is advisable to discuss with family members and make a prudent financial plan to achieve life's goals. It will vary with different life stages and the financial needs will evolve with changes in income levels, increase of expenses, unique requirements of family members, and post-retirement expenses. Some of them are as follows:

- **Single and Earning (Age Group: 20-28)**
  1. Higher education abroad and skill upgradation.
  2. Buying electronic gadgets.
  3. Planning domestic/international vacations with friends.
  4. Having a good investment strategy to build wealth for the future.

- **Early Married Life (Age Group: 28-35)**
  1. Contribution towards household expenses.
  2. Buying a house.
  3. Buying a car.
  4. Investment for future goals.
  5. Higher investment potential due to additional income if the spouse is earning.

- **Married with Kids (Age Group: 35-45)**
  1. Primary and secondary schooling education expenditure.
  2. Debt management for repayment of home loan and car loan.
  3. Vacation planning with family.
  4. Investment planning for wealth accumulation.

- **Middle Age (Age Group: 45-55)**
  1. Sending children abroad for higher education.
  2. Debt management for repayment of the loan.

3. Vacation planning with family.
4. Investment planning for wealth accumulation.
5. Children's marriage planning.

- **Pre-Retirement (Age Group: 55-60)**
  1. Reduction in household expenses as the child is now financially independent.
  2. Investment planning for retirement corpus.
  3. Investment planning for a regular flow of income during retirement.
  4. Relocation and planning for a peaceful retirement.
  5. Estate planning.

- **Post-Retirement (Age Group: 60+)**
  1. Implementing investment strategy for regular retirement income.
  2. Asset allocation on a portfolio with lower risk.
  3. Inheritance and estate planning.
  4. Charity and social work.

- **Single Women**
  1. Self-living expenses.
  2. Support to parents and dependent siblings.
  3. Investment planning.
  4. Retirement corpus.

- **Single Women with Dependent Kids**
    1. Living expenses.
    2. Children's education.
    3. Investment planning.
    4. Retirement corpus.

### 1.3 Risk Appetite

Risk appetite is the combination of ability and willingness of the investor to bear the risk and accept the uncertainty of the outcome. Risk and Return are correlated. The higher the risk, the higher is the likely return. Risk tolerance is an individual psychological trait and impacted by behavioural biases. Risk Appetite is broadly categorized into aggressive, moderate or conservative. Aggressive investors have higher risk tolerance and Conservative investors have lower risk tolerance. Taking a higher risk by a conservative investor creates cognitive dissonance and hence results in loss aversion. Aggressive investors can take market losses in their stride and wait with patience for the market upturn.

It is generally assumed that youngsters, at start of their earning career, are willing to take a risk and have an aggressive risk appetite whereas retired people are less willing to take a risk and have a conservative risk appetite.

## 2. Investment Cycle and Asset Allocation

### 2.1 Strategic Asset Allocation

Strategic asset allocation plays a pivotal role in converting the investor's goals, constraints, risk appetite, and time horizon into an appropriate portfolio. A strategic asset allocation strategy may be akin to a buy-and-hold strategy and suggests diversification to balance between risk and returns. For example, if stocks have historically returned 10% per year and bonds have returned 5% per year, a portfolio with a mix of 50% stocks and 50% bonds would be expected to generate a return of 7.5% per year.

### 2.2 Rebalancing

Even the most carefully constructed portfolios need periodic review. Three areas that require attention from the investor and advisor for monitoring portfolio are changes in:

i. Investor's personal circumstances and wealth.

ii. Market/economic changes.

iii. Changes to portfolio holdings/assets.

Primarily, there are two types of rebalancing—*calendar rebalancing* and *percentage-of-portfolio rebalancing*. Calendar rebalancing involves rebalancing the portfolio to target weights on a periodic basis such as monthly, quarterly, semiannually, or annually. Compared to this, percentage-of-portfolio rebalancing involves setting rebalancing thresholds (trigger points) that define a corridor or tolerance band for the value of that asset class. A rebalancing discipline ensures that the actual portfolio doesn't drift far away from the target asset allocation and assumes more significance in strong bull or strong bear markets.

**2.3 Tactical Asset Allocation**

The market sometimes displays event-based high volatility and sharp movements. In such scenarios, the portfolio requires short-term adjustments to asset-class weights based on th short-term prediction of the relative performance of the asset classes.

For example, let's assume a portfolio has a mix of 50% stocks and 50% bonds. Given a perception of a future short-term extreme uncertainty in the equity market, the asset allocation could be readjusted by decreasing stocks by 10-20% and increasing bonds by 10-20%, for say, a period of six months or so, or till such an important event is over. Thus, the resulting tactical asset allocation could be equity 30-40% and bonds 60-70%. It may be clarified that the tactical asset allocation for the retail investors forms a part of normal rebalancing exercise, if it is carried out at periodical intervals.

### 2.4 Rupee Cost Averaging

Rupee cost averaging strategy is adopted to mitigate market timing risk. It can be implemented through SIP (systematic investment plan), STP (systematic transfer plan), or SWP (systematic withdrawal plan). Such investment techniques are applied to regular purchases in fixed instalments in shares and mutual funds to lower the cost of investments.

### 2.5 Power of Compounding

Compounding is a powerful concept of investing which acts as a multiplier in investment for long-term investors. This is what Albert Einstein calls as 'the eighth wonder of the world'. It essentially means reinvesting the interest which earns further interest. It is important that one leverages the power of compounding by starting to save early in life and invest regularly for long term.

### 2.6 Behaviourally Modified Asset Allocation (BMAA)

Incorporating investor's behavioural traits into investment strategies leads to the construction of *behaviourally modified asset allocation*. BMAA additionally considers the relative wealth of the investor and the nature of the client's biases to readjust that allocation. It also considers whether to moderate or adapt to the investor's biases in order to construct a portfolio the investor can stick with comfortably. Finally, the amount of deviation from the traditional optimal allocation is determined. This is typically done by setting a range in which the asset class can fluctuate. Thus, BMAA integrates both traditional finance (mean-variance optimisation) and behavioural finance (investor's real-life situation) into asset allocation and aims at arriving at the best possible practical asset allocation.

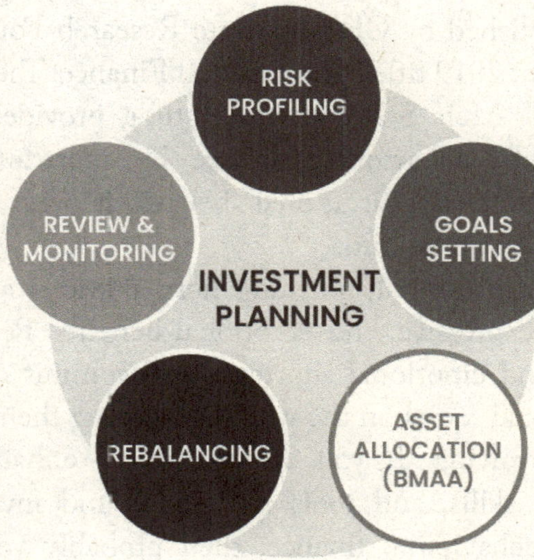


### 3. Future of Behavioural Finance

Behavioural finance (BF) differs from traditional finance in that it focuses on how investors and markets behave in practice rather than in theory. By focusing on actual behaviour, behavioural researchers have observed that individuals make investment decisions in ways and with outcomes that differ from the approaches and outcomes of traditional finance.

During the past 30 years, BF has emerged as a hot topic, generating new credence every day. The investment landscape has been enriched with several brilliant research articles including 'Irrational Exuberance' by Robert Shiller, 'Beyond Greed and Fear: Understanding Behavioural

Finance and the Psychology of Investing' by Hersh Shiffrin, and 'Prospect Theory' by Daniel Kahneman and Amos Tversky, among others. In one of the latest research reports published by CFA Institute Research Foundation in December 2019 titled 'Behavioural Finance: The Second Generation', Meir Statman, the author, provides a new dimension to behavioural finance by substituting the often-quoted phrase 'irrational" behaviour' with 'normal" behaviour'. To quote him:

"People are normal, pursuing normal wants and their utilitarian, expressive, and emotional benefits. People use cognitive and emotional shortcuts and commit cognitive and emotional errors on the way to satisfying their wants."

BF is evolving. If you are excited to enhance your knowledge, skills, and tools in finance and investment, including behavioural finance, then probably you could connect with the CFA Institute, USA, which is the world's largest association of investment professionals (www.cfainstitute.org). One can benefit from the latest research reports and analysis by leading investment professionals around the world and also able to exchange ideas among leading investment experts and practitioners.

## Concluding Remarks

Human beings are born to win. As they grow in life, hereditary and environmental factors influence their thoughts and behaviour. People differ in terms of financial wealth and income. The globalisation of economies and markets results in high volatility, creating fear and anxiety in the mind of investors. The lack of social security, like unemployment allowance or old age pension in India, puts additional focus on the role of financial planning and wealth management.

Please remember that even the wisest of investors has no control over the market outcome. Besides, there is no definite amount of wealth that can bring perfect financial security. A structured and disciplined approach to financial planning and portfolio creation can ensure financial well-being. With clearly defined financial goals and a long-term portfolio, a person with a low level of wealth can lead a better quality of life. At the same time, a person with a high level of wealth without control over one's biases (example, greed and fear), often suffers from stress and anxiety. This is where the basic knowledge of behavioural finance helps. As explained in the book, identifying, managing, and controlling behavioural biases, building a BMAA, and sticking to it in a disciplined manner will most likely ensure investment success in the long term.

Before you finish reading the book, please take a pause. Hold your breath for a few seconds. By doing so, you will realise that one will be dead without breathing air even for a few minutes. That is strikingly simple, but incredible insight. In fact, there are five such elements—*bhūmi* (earth), *jala* (water), *tejas* or *agni* (fire), *marut* (air), and *akash* (space)—that constantly at work inside the human body to keep us alive. And we find the same five elements in the outside nature. Lack or excesses of any one of these elements can cause disaster (example, flood caused due to excess of water and famine due to acute scarcity of water). Having a proper balance of these five elements makes nature beautiful. We can extend the same logic to human life. Mastering the art of balancing different types of wealth, i.e., physical, social, emotional, and financial wealth, will make life healthy, happy, and prosperous. Integrating the investment cycle with a much larger life cycle will make our journey into the future more enjoyable and meaningful.

With this, we have come to the end! Hope this book supports your successful investment journey.

# Annexure: Diagnostic Testing

बन्धुरात्मात्मनस्तस्य येनात्मैवात्मना जतिः ।
अनात्मनस्तु शत्रुत्वे वर्तेत तात्मैव शत्रुवत् ॥
6॥

*"For those who have conquered the mind, it is their friend. For those who have failed to do so, the mind works like an enemy."*

—The Bhagavad Gita

## Suggested strategy to readers of the book

One way of using the book for busy professionals is to first look at the diagnostic questionnaire given below, identify any behavioural bias the reader has, and then read the specific chapter dedicated to such bias. This will help in learning first about one's own bias and then appropriately responding to the correcting or mitigating measures to optimise investments.

## Cognitive Biases

| Name of Biases | Questions | Typical Response Confirming Susceptibility to the Bias (in bold) |
|---|---|---|
| Anchoring and Adjustment Bias | Suppose you bought a car for INR 10,00,000 some three years ago. You would like to buy a new car by disposing the old car. Your car is in a good condition and the normal price expectation of such a car in the market is INR 300,000. Your agent informed you that the prices of second-hand cars have crashed and quotes a price for your car INR 2,00,000. What is your most likely response? | 1. You make an offer to sell your car for INR 2,00,000.<br>2. You make an offer to sell your car for INR 2,50,000.<br>3. **You make an offer to sell your car for INR 2,40,000, i.e., @ 20 per cent higher than the original offer from the agent.** |
| Availability Bias | Suppose you wish to invest in the stock market. You hear about an IPO (initial public offer) in the pharma sector that is being launched. Your neighbour, who is known to have good stock market | 1. I will do my independent research before making the investment.<br>2. I will avoid investment in IPOs as it is a high-risk game. |

| Name of Biases | Questions | Typical Response Confirming Susceptibility to the Bias (in bold) |
|---|---|---|
| | knowledge, recommends you invest in IPO in question. What is your response to this situation? | 3. **I will apply for the IPO without any hesitation because my neighbour is probably correct.** |
| Representativeness Bias | In a cricket match, there is a coin toss at the beginning of the play. The team winning the toss is given the option to bat or field first. The Indian cricket team is playing a series. The Indian captain has lost the toss consecutively in the last two matches. What is the probability of his winning toss in the next match? | 1. 100 per cent.<br>2. 50 per cent.<br>3. **0 per cent.** |
| Framing Bias | You are unwell and need hospitalisation urgently. You have to decide between Lilavati or Beach Candy | 1. **I will choose Lilavati hospital because it has a past record of 97 per cent of patients being cared.** |

| Name of Biases | Questions | Typical Response Confirming Susceptibility to the Bias (in bold) |
|---|---|---|
| | hospital. How would you decide? | 2. **I will go for Beach Candy hospital as it has a record of only 3 per cent of its patients not being cured in the past.**<br>3. I am okay with either Lilavati or Beach Candy hospital. |
| Conservatism Bias | You have invested in in a good stock for many years now. A news comes that has potentially negative implication for the price of the stock. What is your quick response to such a situation? | 1. I will sell the stocks.<br>2. **I will wait for more negative news before selling the stocks.**<br>3. **I have this stock for many years now. I think the company will overcome the negative event.** |
| Confirmation Bias | You have invested in a security after some careful research. You come across a media report that the company you have invested in has a problem with its main product line. However, another report suggests that | 1. I will take notice of the problem and exit the investment.<br>2. **I will take notice of the new product and continue investment till further negative announcement.**<br>3. **Normally, I stick to my investments** |

| Name of Biases | Questions | Typical Response Confirming Susceptibility to the Bias (in bold) |
|---|---|---|
| | a new product will be launched by the company in near future. How would you react to such a situation? | **regardless of news and developments.** |
| Hindsight Bias | You have invested in a security and it increases in value. However, the underlying reasons for your decisions are not reflected in the current price rise. How do you respond to such a situation? | 1. I will try to understand the reasons for price rise and be careful in future.<br>2. **I will be happy that I made a great investment.**<br>3. I will exit the investment. |
| Illusion of Control Bias | You have an above-average success in winning the lottery. What do you mainly attribute this success to? | 1. Pure luck.<br>2. **You are choosing a number the total of which is divisible by 9.**<br>3. You are relying on computer-generated number. |
| Recency Bias | You are a first-time investor and had started investing one year back. Your | 1. **I will exit and never enter the the market again.**<br>2. I will analyse the |

| Name of Biases | Questions | Typical Response Confirming Susceptibility to the Bias (in bold) |
|---|---|---|
| | portfolio corrected by 38% during March 2020 after Covid 19 pandemic event. What will be your future strategy? | past market crashes and learn from them.<br>3. I will take the advice of an expert on investment. |
| Mental Accounting Bias | A. You arrive at a cinema hall to see a film. You realise that you have misplaced your ticket. You had paid for the ticket INR 200. Still, tickets at the same price are available at the counter. Will you purchase another INR 200 ticket to see the show?<br><br>B. You arrive at a cinema hall to see a film. You realise that you lost INR 200 specially kept for the film while travelling in the local train. There is an ATM nearby. Tickets are available at the counter. Will you | 1. **Yes.**<br>2. No.<br><br>1. Yes.<br>2. **No.**<br><br>*If the answer to A and B are different, then mental accounting bias is likely present. |

| Name of Biases | Questions | Typical Response Confirming Susceptibility to the Bias (in bold) |
|---|---|---|
| | make a cash withdrawal and purchase an INR 200 ticket to see the show? | |
| Cognitive Dissonance Bias | Suppose that you recently bought a new car: brand A, model X. You are happy with your purchase. Soon after your purchase, you discover that another car — model Y from the the same brand (model Y is nearly identical to model X) — is giving away a five-year free free motor insurance package when you buy the car. What is likely to be your reaction? | 1. You contact the car dealer to find out more information to ascertain if you missed an opportunity.<br>2. You immediately research some consumer magazines to find out more information about the current trends in discounts and and free gifts.<br>3. **The prospect of discovering an error in your purchase makes you uncomfortable. Hence, you decide to enjoy the car without any further research.** |

## Emotional Biases

| Name of Biases | Questions | Typical Response Confirming Susceptibility to the Bias (in bold) |
|---|---|---|
| Endowment Bias | Assume that your late father has bequeathed to you 5,000 shares of HDFC bank. Your financial advisor tells you to sell a part of HDFC bank shares and diversify into other banks stocks. What is your most likely decision? | 1. I will sell HDFC bank shares and diversify into other banks as advised by my financial advisor.<br>2. **HDFC bank is an an excellent holding. I will not sell these shares despite their recent poor performance.**<br>3. **These shares are a symbol of my father's deep love for me and have provided a good return. I will continue holding these shares.** |
| | You inadvertently purchased 1,000 shares of Nestle. Shortly thereafter, you discovered that you already own 1,000 shares of Nestle in your portfolio. Now the redundant holdings are causing an imbalance in your | 1. I will quickly sell shares of Nestle and correct the imbalance.<br>2. **I have already paid the brokerage and commission towards the purchase of Nestle stock. Hence, I will keep the additional Nestle shares.** |

| Name of Biases | Questions | Typical Response Confirming Susceptibility to the Bias (in bold) |
|---|---|---|
| | portfolio. Selling shares will involve small transaction cost. How do you react to this situation? | 3. I will make a cost-benefit analysis on rebalancing Nestle stocks and then decide. |
| Self-attribution (Self-Serving) Bias | Your investments have gained handsomely since March 2020 after the Covid 19 event. To what do you attribute the success? | 1. Fiscal stimulus by the governments.<br>2. Secular rise of the the markets after event.<br>3. **I have selected good stocks last year.**<br>4. Liquidity infusion by FED and central banks around the world. |
| | You made significant gains from selling DMart shares. How do you deal with the money/sale proceeds? | 1. I will do research and wait until I find another good investment idea.<br>**2. I will make an investment in another e-commerce startup immediately.**<br>3. I will transfer the gain to bank FD. |

| Name of Biases | Questions | Typical Response Confirming Susceptibility to the Bias (in bold) |
|---|---|---|
| Regret Aversion Bias | You have invested in Reliance at INR 1,200. It has appreciated to INR 2,300 during the last 12 months. Your broker advised you to book profit. You come across a news item that Amazon is planning to take an equity stake in Reliance. How do you deal with such a situation? | 1. I will sell the stock regardless of what happens to stock price post sale.<br>2. **I will postpone the trade.**<br>3. I will make further analysis before deciding. |
| | You decide to acquire 1,000 shares of Bharti Airtel at INR 580 per share. You like to wait a few days before picking up the additional 500 shares. Now, soon after your initial buy, the market falls and Bharti Airtel share is now available @ INR 515. There is no change in fundamentals. How do you deal with such a situation? | 1. I will buy the remaining 500 shares INR @ 515.<br>2. **I will wait until the stock begins to go up before buying the remaining 500 shares.**<br>3. I will do further analysis to find out the reasons for the fall and decide appropriately. |

# Annexure: Diagnostic Testing

| Name of Biases | Questions | Typical Response Confirming Susceptibility to the Bias (in bold) |
|---|---|---|
| Status Quo Bias | Which of the following options would you choose? | 1. **A 100 per cent chance of winning INR 100,000.**<br>2. An 80 per cent chance of winning INR 130,000 with a 20 per cent chance of winning nothing.<br>3. A 50 per cent chance of winning INR 210,00 with a 50 per cent chance of winning nothing. |
| | Your investment portfolio contains an an AAA-rated corporate bond. Your advisor has recommended to replace the corporate bond with a newly issued PSU bond with more safety and and better return. You aren't familiar with this PSU bond. What is your most likely decision? | 1. **I am happy with the current investment and will keep things as they are.**<br>2. I will replace AAA corporate bond with a newly issued PSU bond.<br>3. I will analyse further and decide. |

<table>
<tr><th>Name of Biases</th><th>Questions</th><th>Typical Response Confirming Susceptibility to the Bias (in bold)</th></tr>
<tr><td rowspan="2">Overconfidence Bias</td><td>The global financial crisis (GFC) of 2008-09 seriously disrupted many economies and markets. How easy do you think it was to predict GFC?</td><td>1. Difficult.<br>2. Easy.<br>3. Somewhat easy.</td></tr>
<tr><td>Relative to other drivers on the road, how good a a driver are you?</td><td>1. Not so good.<br>2. Average.<br>3. Above average.</td></tr>
<tr><td rowspan="2">Self-Control Bias</td><td>You are overweight for the last 10 years and your body mass index (BMI) is hovering above 30. What will be your action plan?</td><td>1. I will consult a a dietician for my daily diets and take a membership of a gym.<br>2. I have been following the right plans for the last 10 years but find it difficult to accomplish target set by me.<br>3. I do everything to stay fit and ensure annual health check-ups.</td></tr>
<tr><td>You are 50 years of age and plan to retire after 10 years. What will be your action plan for retirement corpus?</td><td>1. There is enough time to think about this.<br>2. I am saving through EPF and the amounts will take of my retirement needs.</td></tr>
</table>

| Name of Biases | Questions | Typical Response Confirming Susceptibility to the Bias (in bold) |
|---|---|---|
| | | 3. I realise it is time to visit a financial planner to draw my action plan. |
| Optimism Bias | You have been investing in real estate over the last 20 years and have made good profits. You advise others to invest in real estate. How do you rate yourself relative to other investors? | 1. Below Average.<br>2. **Above average.**<br>3. Average. |
| | How optimistic are you about the investing opportunities close to to home versus those overseas? | 1. I am much more optimistic about investment opportunities close to home.<br>2. I am more optimistic about investment opportunities in foreign locations compared to those available in my home country.<br>3. I am neutral between investment opportunities close to home and in foreign locations. |

| Name of Biases | Questions | Typical Response Confirming Susceptibility to the Bias (in bold) |
|---|---|---|
| Loss Aversion Bias | Suppose you have invested in a stock that has gradually fallen 25% in value in the last six months. Most of the brokers have 'neutral' or 'hold' rating. You are unsure whether the stock will recover. What will you do? | 1. I will sell the stock at a loss and hold cash.<br>2. **I will hold on to the stock because it is better to wait till the stock recovers.**<br>3. I will sell at a loss and look for better investment ideas. |
| | Suppose you have made an initial investment of INR 100,000. You are required to choose from three alternative scenarios. How would you likely proceed? | 1. **Receive INR 90,000 for sure.**<br>2. Take a 50-50 probability—you either get back INR 120,000 or INR 80,000.<br>3. Take an 80-20 probability—you get back either INR 80,000 or INR 180,000. |

# Acknowledgements

Our sincere thanks to Mr G. N. Bajpai, a visionary leader spearheading socio-economic transformation in India for many decades. As the head of several organisations, including the Securities and Exchange Board of India (SEBI) and Life Insurance Corporation of India (LIC), he has been instrumental for reforms and innovations in major financial sectors that includes insurance, pension, and capital markets. We are grateful to him for the foreword.

We would like to thank Mr Navneet Munot (CFA, managing director and CEO, HDFC Asset Management Co Ltd) for being a source of inspiration to bring out this book. We thank Mr Gajendra Kothari (CFA, managing director and CEO, Etica Wealth Pvt Ltd) for providing valuable feedback on the book.

Our special thanks to Mr Biswarup Mohapatra CFA for his useful inputs while writing the book.

A big thank you to all our clients for helping us with insights into various behavioural biases affecting investment decisions. We are also indebted to Sonali Praharaj, an architect based in Toronto, for her incisive and diligent work in compiling the book.

Finally, we would like to thank our parents, teachers, spouses, family members, school and college friends, colleagues in offices, and our clients for educating us about our behaviours, blind spots, and thinking errors.

Last but not the least, we thank the readers. We eagerly look forward to receiving feedback.

Prakash Praharaj and Nirakar Pradhan

# References


1. Chandra Prasanna. *Investment Analysis and Portfolio Management*. Publisher: Tata McGraw-Hill, New Delhi.
2. CFA Institute Research and Analysis. Future of Finance. The CFA Institute (www.cfainstitute.org/en/research/future-finance).
3. Government of India: Economic Survey-2020 (www.indiabudget.gov.in/economicsurvey).
4. Kahneman Daniel and Tversky Amos: Prospect Theory. Chapter 6. *Handbook of The Fundamentals of Financial Decision Making*. Publisher: World Scientific Publishing Co. NJ, USA.
5. Kahneman Daniel: Nobel Prize Winner. *Thinking Fast and Slow* by Daniel Kahneman. Publisher: FSG Adult, New York, USA (2013).
6. National Stock Exchange (www.nseindia.com).
7. Pompian, Michael CFA, CFP. *Behavioural Finance and Wealth Management*. Publisher: John Wiley & Sons, Canada.
8. Pompian, Michael and John Longo. 2005. 'Incorporating Behavioural Finance into Your Practice'. Journal of Financial Planning. Vol.18. no. 3. page: 58-63.
9. Reserve Bank of India: Annual Handbook of Statistics on Indian Economy (www.rbi.org.in).
10. Richards Carl. 2012. *The Behaviour Gap: Simple Ways to Stop Doing Dumb Things with Money*. Publisher: Penguin Books Ltd. UK.

11. Sadhguru Jaggi Vasudev. *Mind is Your Business*. Publisher: Diamond Books, New Delhi.
12. Shefrin Hersh. *Beyond Greed and Fear: Understanding Behavioural Finance and the Psychology of Investing*. Publisher: OUP, USA (2002).
13. Shiller Robert. *Irrational Exuberance*. Publisher: Princeton University Press, NJ, USA.
14. Statman Meir. *Behavioural Finance: The Second Generation*. Publisher: CFA Institute Research Foundation, USA (2019).
15. Thaler Richard H. and Sunstein Cass R. *Nudge*. Publisher: Penguin Books, UK.
16. World Bank: GDP and GDP per capita (www.tradingeconomics.com).

**Prakash Praharaj**, M.Com (Gold Medalist), CAIIB, CFP$^{CM}$

Mr Praharaj is the author of *Your Everyday Guide to Personal Finance and Insurance* published by CNBC TV 18. He has been awarded two gold medals for securing top positions both in graduation and post-graduation in commerce. He is an MBA, ICWA(I), CAIIB, DTIRM (diploma in treasury, investment, and risk management), a Certified Financial Planner$^{CM}$ (affiliated to FPSB, Denver), and certificate holder on behavioural science from University of Berkeley, USA. He is also a fee-only financial planner', a SEBI registered investment advisor, and founder of Max Secure Financial Planners.

He has working experience of more than 30 years with Reserve Bank of India, United India Insurance Co, State Bank of India, and SBI Life Insurance Co. He has worked in the treasury department of SBI and as chief risk officer of SBI Life Insurance Company. He has also been a visiting professor of finance at ITM (Vashi), IIBM (Sanpada), and IBSAR and has conducted financial well-being programs in corporates and institutions in association with Network FP Knowledge Solutions Pvt Ltd.

He has published articles in various newspapers including The Mint Money, The Financial Express, The Economic Times, The Business Bhaskar, and The Indian Express and has a blog where he writes about various topics pertaining to financial planning. He is also engaged in spreading financial literacy and has taken preparatory sessions for school students in Navi Mumbai for NFLAT (National Financial Literacy Assessment Tests). He also provides comprehensive financial planning and investment advisory service and has helped many people in organising their financial life by undertaking financial life planning for them.

**Dr Nirakar Pradhan**, Ph.D, CFA, FRM

Nirakar holds a Ph.D in Business Administration from Utkal University, India and is a CFA charter holder, certified financial risk manager from GARP, USA, certified credit research analyst, and Certified Financial Planner$^{CM}$.

He has over 30 years of experience in the financial sector in India and Europe, focusing on banking, insurance, credit, investment, portfolio management, and enterprise risk management. He led many high performing teams in State Bank of India (India's largest Bank) and Generali Group (a leading European player in Insurance and capital markets). He is especially recognised for his investment and portfolio management skills, having managed investments for institutional clients over the last two decades.

His previous assignments include head of investment control at Generali Investments (Paris, 2015-17), chief investment officer at Future Generali India Life Insurance Company Limited (Mumbai, 2008-2014), head of Investments at SBI (Frankfurt, 2003-07), and head of treasury at SBI Gilts, now DFHI (Mumbai 1998-2002).

He is currently chief executive officer, India, for PRMIA (Professional Risk Managers' International Association), a USA based professional association dedicated to promoting education and training in financial risk management. He is also the founder of Fin Kasturi Nivesh Private Limited, a SEBI registered investment advisor. A multi-lingual communicator, Nirakar takes a keen interest in promoting financial education, innovation, and best market practices through conferences, media, industry, regulators, and academic institutions.